GOD HELP ME!

This **stress** is driving me crazy

GOD HELP ME!

This **stress** is driving me crazy

Finding BALANCE through God's Grace

GREGORY K. POPCAK

LOYOLAPRESS.

CHICAGO

LOYOLAPRESS.

3441 N. ASHLAND AVENUE
CHICAGO, ILLINOIS 60657

Interior and cover design by Megan Duffy Rostan

Library of Congress Cataloging-in-Publication Data
Popcak, Gregory K.
   God help me! this stress is driving me crazy!: finding balance through God's grace / Gregory K. Popcak
      p. cm.
   ISBN 0-8294-1788-5
   1. Peace of mind—Religious aspects—Christianity. 2. Stress (Psychology)—Religious aspects—Christianity. I. Title.
   BV4908.5 .P67 2003
   248.8'6—dc21

                                              2002014374

Printed in the United States of America
02 03 04 05 06 Bang 10 9 8 7 6 5 4 3 2 1

To my family. I love you.

Contents

1

What, Me Worry?

Have no anxiety at all, but in everything, by prayer and
petition, with thanksgiving, make your requests known to God.

(PHILIPPIANS 4:6)

Crazy schedules, conflicting responsibilities, never-ending
piles of work and bills. Complicated relationships, ghosts
from the past, and the feeling that we're being pulled in a zillion
different directions. Sometimes it seems as though life intends to
squeeze us until we pop!

In the eye of the mental hurricane, however, there is a constant, quiet voice calling to the center of our souls. "O my child,"
says the gentle, loving whisper, "you are busy with many things. Be
still. Do not be afraid. I am with you."

Sadly, many of us doubt that God really cares about our everyday
anxieties. We think that the God who has numbered the hairs on our
heads is too busy solving wars, famines, floods, and the million or so
other "real" problems in the world to be concerned with our silly

1

concerns. Shouldn't we just "offer it up" and get over our whiny selves?

Not entirely. While there certainly is merit, as the Apostle Paul says in Colossians, in joining our sufferings with Christ's cross for the good of the church, this does not mean that God does not wish to deliver us from our anxieties. Jesus reminds us that just as earthly parents want to give good things to their children, our heavenly Father—whose love is more perfect and profound than anything we could experience on this earth—wants to shower his goodness upon us. What parents want their child to be consumed with worry? When Jesus' disciples began fretting, "What shall we eat? What shall we drink? What shall we put on today?" Jesus comforted them, confident in the providence of his Father: "Do not worry . . . but seek first the kingdom [of God] and his righteousness, and all these things will be given you besides" (Matthew 6:25, 33).

In the two thousand years since Christ walked the earth, the church has continued to echo this sentiment, from Paul's proclaiming (from prison, no less) that we should not allow anxiety to disturb our minds, all the way through to the modern age. Every time I go to Mass, I hear these words: "Deliver us, Lord, from every evil, and grant us peace in our day. In your mercy, keep us free from sin and protect us from all anxiety as we wait in joyful hope for the coming of our Savior, Jesus Christ."

To me, these powerful words represent both a prayer and a promise for every Christian. Yet this is an extraordinary thing to pray. Protect us from *all* anxiety? Isn't that selfish or, at the very least, hopelessly unrealistic? How many of us can even tie our shoes in the morning without experiencing some small pang of anxiety? Dare we ask the Lord to deliver us from something that is as much a part of daily life as breathing?

The church deems this prayer to be so important that she inserts it into an extraordinarily exalted place—smack-dab in the middle of the Lord's Prayer! It comes right after "and deliver us from evil" and before "for the Kingdom." Do you think, maybe, the church is trying to tell us something?

Paradise Lost

To understand what these words mean, and why we pray them, we need to examine God's original blueprint for the world and humankind. We know what our experience *is*, but it is a Christian's job to strive for what God *intended* the world to be and means for it to be again. To do this, we need to go back to the beginning. In the creation story, we see that it was the Lord's intention to create a harmonious world in which all creatures were at peace in him. And the Lord said, "It is good," as he stopped to rest and consider the wonders his hand had brought forth. In this paradise, there was nothing to fear. Providence and peace ruled the land in which the Lord took his daily stroll.

Then it happened. Sin entered the world, and with it, stress, pain, toil, and, yes, anxiety—all things that continue to plague us to the present.

In paradise before the Fall there was work, but it was not a source of stress. Presumably our first parents had to at least gather the food they ate, and Genesis tells us that human beings were created in part to fill the need to "till the soil" (Genesis 2:5). But they were not anxious about this work. Why should they be? The Lord provided all that they needed, and all they had to do was collect it. Work, yes, but a joyful work, work that contained the assurance of a happy end. They were confident that whatever the day brought, the Lord would provide.

Scripture also tells us that Adam and Eve were "naked, yet they felt no shame" (Genesis 2:25). This is a very significant phrase. Ultimately, it refers to nakedness on a spiritual and psychological level, a level that reveals the total, joyful, vulnerable intimacy our first parents had with their God. They were completely dependent on the Lord and happy to be so. This "nakedness" allowed Adam and Eve to enjoy true peace and confidence even in the face of Evil.

I am willing to wager a large sum that if you were approached by the personification of Evil in the form of a talking snake (even if it was just a metaphorical one), you would most likely break a few speed records in your haste to get out of there. Remarkably though, the story has the pre-fallen Eve standing in the face of Evil incarnate, completely naked and unafraid. Because she was in complete union with God, she could stand casually, innocently, and peacefully before the keeper of the keys to hell without so much as a fig leaf to defend her. Talk about chutzpah!

But after the Fall, Scripture tells us, everything changed. Adam and Eve were ashamed of the nakedness that represented their total, vulnerable dependence on the Lord. They hid. As Pope John Paul II writes, "The necessity of hiding themselves indicates that in the depths of the shame they both feel before each other, as the immediate fruit of the tree of the knowledge of good and evil, there has matured a sense of fear before God: a fear previously unknown."[1]

As it develops, this estrangement from God and resultant fear causes our protoparents to take matters into their own hands. Suddenly, they are afraid—no, terrified—because the world is bigger than they are. How will they cope? What will they eat? What will they drink? What will they put on today? How will they defend themselves against Evil? Satan made good on his promise to Adam and Eve. Suddenly, they had acquired the knowledge of good and evil, the intimate knowledge of what it could mean to have and to have not, to be fulfilled and to be without, not just temporally but

---

[1] Pope John Paul II, *Theology of the Body Part 2*.

relationally, emotionally, and spiritually. And the *knowledge of the possibility of loss* scared them to death, literally, as Scripture tells us that death entered the world on the heels of sin.

Let's bring this discussion a little closer to home. Consider for a moment what causes you stress. What gives you anxiety? For most people, it is the fear of loss. What if I lose my security? What if I lose my spouse's love? What if I lose my freedom? What if I lose my position, my status, my home, my life? It is the knowledge that everything *could* be lost and that we are too tiny, too pathetic, and too powerless to do anything about it that, over the course of a life-time, scares each and every one of us to death.

Paradise Regained

MICHAEL, A FORTY-SIX-YEAR-OLD sales consultant, couldn't sleep nights because of the anxiety he encountered in his work. "I feel like I can never rest. It's extremely competitive at my office. If you don't make the cut, you're out. I've been there for almost twelve years, and still, every day I worry where my next sale will come from. If I don't scramble all the time, someone else is waiting to take that client's business, and I'll have to answer to my manager for it. I love what I do, but the pressure is really getting to me. It's affecting my marriage, my kids, even my health with these headaches I get, but I'm stuck. I make a good living. I'm afraid to change things now. It isn't as if anyone is going to bail me out."

———

LYDIA WAS CONSTANTLY WORRIED about what other people thought of her. She never felt she was good enough and constantly questioned her worth. "The other day, my son's school was asking for volunteers to help with a fundraising project. I wanted to do it, but I just felt like, 'Who am I? I don't have anything to contribute.' I get nervous when I have to take on new things. What if I mess up? Then all those people would be disappointed in me. I never finished college. So many people are so much more talented than I am. Sometimes I feel like God wants me to do more in my life, but I think he'd be better off picking somebody else who knew what they were doing. I'm just a nervous wreck."

———————

In the post-fallen world in which we live, we constantly face the possibility of loss. The only realistic response we can make is to be anxious. But if this is your experience of the "real world," then I have good news for you. *This perception is not the reality.* The experience that passes as "reality" for most people is only a dark, distorted image of the authentic "real world" that Jesus Christ came to restore to us. It is only what we see when, as St. Paul says, "we see indistinctly, as in a mirror" (1 Corinthians 13:12).

But we can only find our way back to the world as God intended it to be if we take Eden as our model. When Jesus was asked about his position on divorce, he appealed to a new authority. He said, "Because of the hardness of your hearts Moses allowed you to divorce your wives, but from the beginning it was not so" (Matthew 19:8). Jesus did not appeal to the law of Moses, which was designed to accommodate the fallenness of humanity. He appealed to the authority of "from the beginning," that is, the way God the Father created the world to be before it fell.

To put it another way, Christ's message to us is that in order to follow him we must rebuild our lives, our relationships, and the world according to God's original blueprint, not some imperfect compromise manufactured in the post-fallen world. This is extremely important to us because God's original plan for humanity did not include anxiety.

The even more remarkable implication is that God would not ask us to do anything that was impossible—difficult, yes; impossible, no. What we are left with is no less a personage than the Son of God telling us that we can—no, must—see Eden as the model for our lives, that anxiety is not a necessary part of the human condition as God intended it, and that God will give us the grace to leave behind this fallen, fearful state.

Jesus came both to open the gates of heaven and to give us the grace to begin rebuilding Eden here on earth. If you are building a house, looking at the pile of lumber and the big hole in the ground won't tell you what to do next. Doing that will only make you anxious. If you want to know which piece of lumber to pick up first, you have to look at the blueprint. Jesus, the new Adam, came to give us the blueprint to a new Eden, one in which human beings are intimately united with God once again for all of eternity. And in this union, there is no room for anxiety.

Jesus came to deliver us from the fear that obscures our vision of the real world, the real world his Father created, the authentic world in which we can be joyfully confident in the providence of our loving Father no matter what we experience in life. Time and again Jesus told us, "Be not afraid." "Why are you anxious?" "If you only had the faith of a mustard seed . . ." "Fear not! I am with you!"

Jesus came to shine his light of truth on the real world. Now, instead of a dark, frightening distorted reflection, we can see the world clearly and brightly as God created it to be. In this real world, this new Eden that is both already present but not yet fulfilled, we have nothing to fear, not even death. As Romans 8:28 tells us, "We know that all things work for good for those who love God, who are called according to his purpose." In the real world, the world that belongs to anyone who loves God, we should not fear anything—not the loss of our security, our peace, our status, even our lives. The person who is living in the spirit of Christ is not afraid, because as Scripture tells us, "For his [Christ's] sake I have accepted the loss of all things and I consider them so much rubbish, that I may gain Christ" (Philippians 3:8).

Why? First, because in Christ we have attained eternal life and nothing can destroy us. Second, because we cannot fail in this life if our eyes are on the Lord. We may suffer, but we will not give out. We may face problems, but we will overcome them. Scripture says, "If God is for us, who can be against us?" (Romans 8:31). Even if we stumble, we will not fall, because God will catch us and stand us up. As the psalmist says, "For God commands the angels / to guard you in all your ways. / With their hands they shall support you, / lest you strike your foot against a stone" (Psalm 91:11–12).

Who's in Charge?

"But Greg," you may say, "isn't this pie-in-the-sky, hopeless, sappy optimism?" Well, it could be. If you interpret these Scriptures to mean that as Christians we can just stick our heads in the sand and pretend that suffering isn't real, then yes, it is sappy Pollyanna thinking. But we can look at the Scriptures and be confident that things will always work out for our good. Because while the struggle is up to us, the ending is written by God. As Christians, we are not responsible for making it happen on our own power; we are simply responsible for getting up every day, walking through the next chapter in the story of our lives, reflecting on and responding to the things that happen to us, and trusting that God will keep turning the pages until we can see for ourselves that all this really is working out for the good.

I know nothing about mountain climbing, and being an arts-and-letters type, the most athletic thing I have done in recent memory is to *read* about sports. Even so, if I were going to climb a mountain, and I had ten extremely strong, seasoned climbers with me—people who knew my weaknesses and were fully prepared to get me to the top no matter what—then I would not be afraid. It would be a struggle for me to reach the summit. It would be a challenge to test my limits, but I would not be truly anxious. I would know that no matter how hard things became, my life was in very good, qualified hands. Under these circumstances, the challenge might even be fun!

On the other hand, it would be a different story if I didn't trust my guides or if I doubted their strength. If that were the case, I would be too terrified to take the first step. Yet even then, the cause of my anxiety would not be the struggle itself, but my doubt, my lack of trust.

In the mountain climb of life, God is my guide, and his angels and the saints surround me at all times, whispering advice and encouragement, righting me when I stumble, carrying me when I am too tired to go on myself. If I give in to anxiety, it will not be because the struggle is too hard, but because I close my eyes to the help around me.

What I've Learned the Hard Way

I want to tell you a little bit about my own struggle with anxiety, because I want you to understand that I, like you, am a work in progress. I have experienced many difficult times in my life, but I remember one year in particular that seemed like my own personal hell. My wife was so sick we feared she was going to die. She could not keep down food, had little energy, and was in constant pain, yet no one could tell us what was wrong. We spent our anniversary in the emergency room because she was so dehydrated from two weeks of uncontrollable vomiting that she needed an IV. Later we joked that I had taken her to the most expensive restaurant in town ($400 for two bags of saline), but at the time there was little to laugh about.

She bore her sufferings like a saint and did as much as her health would allow, but I was forced to attend to almost all of the responsibilities of keeping the house, caring for the children, paying the bills, and managing and running my counseling practice, in addition to doing what little I could to ease her suffering. Because we lived away from family, we had next to no help.

To make matters worse, my business seemed to be failing. In addition to running my own small private practice, I was contracting therapy services to a psychiatrist who had run afoul of the IRS, unbeknownst to me. I counted on this contract work to even out the natural ups and downs of the number of patients from my therapy practice census. One day, without notice, this doctor told me he was closing his office and would be unable to pay me for nearly $30,000 of services that I had provided. A lawsuit would be useless not just because I really couldn't afford an attorney, but also because I would have to stand in line behind at least four other state and federal agencies that wanted money from him as well.

Simultaneously, the publisher who had bought my first secular book went bankrupt before they published my book, and the bankruptcy court judge refused to return the rights of the book to me because they were considered assets that could be sold to another publisher. I had been hoping that somehow my royalties would carry us through the financial mess I was in. Without publication, there would be no royalties.

That same year, our well collapsed. Twice. We couldn't cook, wash, or do anything else having to do with water for two separate weeks. In six months' time, we threw about $5,000 that we didn't have into a hole in the ground—literally—and we still hadn't finished paying off the loan for the first well.

I felt totally alone and in danger of losing everything. I was more scared than I had ever been in my life. I kept looking jealously at our friends because it seemed as though every time they got into some pickle, their parents were there to bail them out with a substantial loan or gift. I was angry because no one was there to do this for us. I was so sick with stress that I began to fear that I might be developing colon cancer since I couldn't seem to eat anything without becoming violently ill. Of course, I couldn't afford to see a doctor and find out.

I couldn't make my wife well, I couldn't make my business work, I couldn't keep my head up anymore. Everything was dry. I would pray and get nothing. But as I look back on this truly terrible time, I see that the worst part of it all was the pain I inflicted on myself in the form of Anxiety. I allowed all the things that were happening to me to shake my faith in God.

I used to believe all the things I was preaching to you a few pages back. I used to live by the motto "If God is for us, who can be against us?" Up to that point I had accomplished a lot for a young man because I refused to believe in the possibility of failure. I knew that I would have to struggle in life and that the struggle was my part in fulfilling God's plan for my life. But I also believed that as long as I kept discerning and struggling, God's will would not be frustrated. He would multiply my pathetic efforts as he multiplied the loaves and the fishes. As Paul says, God's glory would be revealed in my weakness (see 2 Corinthians 12:9).

I never doubted this, and these beliefs had always seemed to work for me. Every day I would seek God's help and counsel with every decision. No matter how hard things got, I kept at it because

I believed that God would not let me fail. My prayer had always been, "Lord, just let me do your will. Show me which way to go." And then I would get up and do whatever he put in front of me, no matter how crazy it seemed to me or anyone else. I had prayed this prayer every day for at least twenty years, and it helped me choose my career, my wife, where I lived, everything. I had never felt really hopeless or fearful to my core, because I believed that as long as I kept discerning God's will for my life and persevering, God and I could overcome any obstacle that was put in our path.

But through that crushing year, I allowed the anxiety to take hold. I decided that I had been foolish in thinking that I had discerned correctly for all those years. God was punishing me for my folly. I decided that for all that time what I had told myself was my confidence in him was just my pride, my childish belief in my own indestructibility. Who did I think I was anyway? It was time to grow up, to put aside those childish beliefs and face the facts. Life was hard. There wasn't anything I could do about it, and there wasn't anything God was going to do about it.

In my fear, I decided that God was trying to teach me that it was my job to suffer without question until the day he crushed me totally. Again, who did I think I was to presume that he could love me? What was I anyway? I became so consumed with anxiety and fear and doubt that I couldn't discern anything. I slogged through each day, becoming more depressed and fearful (all the while, ironically, counseling other people through their fears and depressions).

I kept praying that God would deliver me, but as each day came and deliverance seemed further away, I started to doubt that God wanted to be my father. Maybe those people who said God only watches us from a distance but doesn't get involved had been right all along. Maybe things had worked out for me so far because I was lucky, and now my luck had run out. Maybe God really did want me to suffer for some mysterious reason that I could never know.

Somehow God kept me going, and as time went by, he began to show me why he had allowed those things to happen to me. Through the anxiety, we finally connected, and I saw the path through the shadows. As I began walking on the path he was pushing me toward, the pain lessened and healing occurred—healing of body, spirit, and finances. I came to see that all along God had been leading me down a path that was narrow and hard, but if I had just trusted him, I could have walked it unafraid. He wanted to lead me to greener pastures, but I fought him all the way, like a child who twists and wiggles as his parent tries to hold his hand in busy traffic.

"No, God! I don't want to go there. I like it here! What will become of me if I go down that road?" I wanted a nice, normal, successful life that was entirely within my ability to control. God wanted to show me that I never really was in control. He was. He always will be.

And because God is in control, I don't have to worry about living in a world that is too big for me. All I have to do is get up in the morning and do the work he puts in front of me, and he will handle the rest. And, having arrived at this place to which he had to drag me kicking and screaming, I am more content than I could have dreamed possible.

I still struggle, and there are days that are difficult to bear. There are still bills to pay and health issues that are controlled but must be monitored, but even in the struggle I am content because I am working at fulfilling the purpose for which I was created. I could not discover my purpose on my own; only God could lead me here, just as he will lead me to the next thing he wants me to do. But from now on, I vow to trust that his will is good. I will seek to fulfill that will with the confidence that no matter how hard I must struggle, I will not fail with Christ who strengthens me.

It's All Still True

Since this epiphany, my family and I have been through other hardships and trials, some quite serious. But I have worked at never allowing myself to give in to the same anxiety, and therefore the pain has never been as bad. When I go through hard times, I remember that all those things I believed are still true. Let me summarize them here for you.

1. **God is our personal father and provider.** He loves us, and all things will work to our ultimate good if we love and trust him first. As Scripture says, "Seek first the kingdom [of God] and his righteousness, and all these things will be given you besides" (Matthew 6:33).

2. **It is not our job to make it all work.** It is only our job to do the best we can, to discern and to struggle and to trust that the ending is in God's loving hands. Above all, we must remember that that ending will be something that we experience as good once we get there.

3. **On the road we may suffer.** We may experience loss. But this is only because God is taking something away from us so that he can lead us to the resurrection after the cross. Just remember that in order to arrive at this resurrection, we must not sit and despair, but discern, struggle, trust, and step out in faith. If we do not do these things, his will and our joy will be obscured by anxiety.

4. **We were created by God to do a particular work.** When something functions according to the purpose for which it

was created, it is healthy and content. God will not contra-
dict his purpose. He will not ask us to do a work for which
we were not created. Therefore, we can trust that his will for
our lives will cause us to be the people we were created to
be. By this process, we will come to celebrate the joy of the
Lord and the peace beyond all understanding.

5. **We can't be afraid that the obstacles that stand between us
   and the fulfillment of our purpose are too great.** If we are
   struggling to follow what we prayerfully believe is God's
   will for our lives, he will multiply our efforts as he multiplied the loaves and fishes, so that the world can marvel
   at how much God can accomplish with so little.

6. **We cannot pursue happiness on our own.** Because we
   cannot see reality, but only a dark reflection of it, many of
   the things we think will make us happy will ultimately
   hurt or destroy us. The more we try to find our own happiness, the more anxious we will become, because we cannot
   find what will make us happy or because we constantly fear
   losing it. If we want to be happy and free from anxiety, we
   must trust that God will help us discover our purpose and,
   ultimately, our contentment in that purpose.

The Possible Dream

Overcoming anxiety is more than a possible dream; it is a central
tenet of Christian spirituality. In his book *Spiritual Passages*, psychologist and spiritual director Fr. Benedict Groeschel examines the
lives of the saints to map the stages of spiritual maturity as well as

the psychological milestones of that journey. He observes that as one progresses through the Purgative Way (in which one routs out sinful and destructive ways of living), the Illuminative Way (in which one begins to achieve a new level of wisdom), and the Unitive Way (in which one achieves an intimate, almost marital union with God), one experiences an increase in trust and a decrease in anxiety.

Throughout the Purgative Way, anxiety is still stronger than our trust of God's love, but it decreases day by day as we strive to overcome our destructive patterns, faulty thoughts, and spiritual sloth. One day, we wake up and cross the threshold of the Illuminative Way, the point at which the experience of trust begins to consistently outweigh the experience of fear and anxiety. While there is still much growth ahead and many pitfalls to avoid, the experience of trust and peace only increases as we move down this spiritual pathway toward the loving arms of the God who, like the father of the prodigal son, runs to meet us on the road back to him.

Groeschel's book confirms my own professional and personal observations that freedom from anxiety is not just reserved for the high and the mighty. It is a gift given by God to all those who would seek him with a sincere heart and a steadfast spirit.

It has been said that the church is not a museum of saints, but a hospital for sinners. The one thing that all sinners suffer from, and that saints do not—at least to the same degree—is anxiety. Walking the path away from anxiety and toward what Scripture calls "the peace of God that surpasses all understanding" (Philippians 4:7) is part of a long healing process. To successfully complete our course of therapy, we are going to need a treatment plan, the latest technologies available, and the love and encouragement of good friends.

While the Scriptures and our spiritual heritage will be our treatment plan, over the next few chapters I will present some psychological skills and spiritual techniques that will help to build up our mental immune systems, increase our spiritual muscle mass, and ultimately help us achieve our maximum therapeutic potential under the watchful eye of the Divine Physician. Likewise, I will share some of my experiences and the experiences of men and women with whom I have been privileged to work over the years to offer you some companionship and comfort in your recovery.

Everyone comes to this "hospital" with a different level of woundedness, and the best treatment always starts with a good evaluation of the severity of the problem. Some people are consumed with fears and anxieties. Their lives are a train wreck, and the wounds they suffer are like serious internal bleeding that causes them to fear as if for their lives. Others, while not overcome with fear, are like patients dealing with chronic pain that they have learned to live with. Still others are basically healthy people, but from time to time they get walloped with a nasty bout of the flu, causing them to panic as they are thrust into situations beyond their control.

As we begin, I would like to do a little bit of triage. Take the following quiz in order to assess the degree to which anxiety has infected your soul. Answer "True" or "False" next to each statement.

HOW MUCH ANXIETY DO YOU FEEL?

____ I feel overwhelmed by my life.

____ I feel there isn't enough of me to go around.

____ I frequently worry about things beyond my control.

____ Even the littlest problem causes me to be overcome with worry or despair.

____ I often worry about problems that don't end up happening.

____ I have a hard time saying no to people who ask me to do things that I don't have the time or energy to do.

____ I often second-guess myself and wonder after the fact if I should have done something differently or better.

____ I have difficulty trusting God to take care of me in the practical matters of everyday life.

____ I feel as if it is up to me to make everything work out, because no one can or will help me.

____ I often compare myself to other people and find that I am not as intelligent/talented/attractive/worthwhile/interesting as they are.

____ When something bad happens to someone else, I worry that that same thing might happen to me.

____ I frequently feel exhausted or overwhelmed by the problems I encounter in my day.

____ I often worry about losing the things that are important to me.

____ I often worry about the people I love dying, becoming ill, or leaving me.

____ I often worry about dying or becoming ill.

____ People tell me I worry too much.

____ It is hard for me to be playful or joyful because of all the problems I have to deal with.

____ When I have a problem, I become obsessed with it and can't stop thinking about it until it is resolved.

____ I believe that God loves me in a personal way, but I have a hard time feeling it.

____ It is difficult for me to relax, even if I am doing something enjoyable.

Scoring

Score one point for each statement you marked "True."

0–2 Very good. You appear to have exceptional strategies for managing your stress. Read on with an eye toward reinforcing your strengths.

3–6 Fair. You have an average amount of anxiety, but it may often get the best of you. As you read, look for new strategies that will help you arm yourself better against the stresses of daily living so that you can experience more joy.

7+ Poor. You have an ongoing struggle with stress that may be both pervasive and endemic. Pay close attention to both the techniques and mental attitudes presented in this book. You need to rework not only your behavior but also the underlying belief system that sustains your stress. Counseling may be indicated.

Whatever your score, I want to encourage you that there is hope. Remember, Scripture tells us that we "have the strength for everything through him who empowers" us (Philippians 4:13). We can overcome the stress demons that seek to steal our joy and obscure our path in the hope of preventing us from becoming the people God created us to be.

As you read on, remember that if we were created for a purpose, then God will not let that purpose be frustrated. All we must do is seek his will, struggle to fulfill as Scripture says, "the ways of your heart, / the vision of your eyes" (Ecclesiastes 11:9), and trust that even though the ending is beyond our control it is well within God's control. As it says in Habakkuk, "The vision still has its time, / presses on to fulfillment, and will not disappoint; / If it delays, wait for it" (Habakkuk 2:3).

God has made each of us a promise: we do not have to fear if we love him. In the next chapter, we will begin to unpack the tools that will allow us to put this promise into practice. As you read on, I encourage you to stand on this promise as your firm foundation, a promise confirmed in the Word of God and echoed by his church for more than two thousand years: "Be not afraid!"

2

The Song of the Siren

Early Greek mythology told of beautiful creatures called Sirens—half women and half birds—who sang magical songs and caused unwary seamen to run their ships aground on the rocky coasts of far-flung islands. Odysseus, you may recall, plugged his sailors' ears with wax and had them tie him to the ship's mast so he alone could hear the Sirens' song but not succumb.

We must contend with latter-day Sirens, whose songs are no less alluring or dangerous. One of these modern Sirens is Anxiety. *How can that be?* you may wonder. *How could we be duped by something as unattractive as Anxiety?* We saw in the last chapter that anxiety was not a part of God's original plan for humanity and that God, through the person of Jesus Christ, calls us to return to our pre-fallen state by means of his grace and our own struggle against our fallen selves. So, knowing the havoc that anxiety can bring, how could we be tempted to do anything but run hastily in the other direction from its siren song?

Like the Sirens, Anxiety makes itself appear as something it is not. It wears a beautiful mask and calls itself Prudence. In a silky voice it whispers, "A little stress keeps you sharp. It helps you anticipate problems. It motivates you! Why, if you let go of *all* the anxiety in your life, you'd never do anything. You'd be a slug."

Look at the creation story again. In it, we have the serpent tempting Eve to flout the one request God has made of her and her husband: "You shall not eat it [the fruit of the tree in the middle of the garden] or even touch it, lest you die" (Genesis 3:3). Eve does not wish to disobey God; after all, God cautioned her that if she does, she will die. She understands that as far as her Creator Father is concerned, there is some great personal risk that accompanies her disobedience.

But the serpent tries to convince her that he is actually doing her a favor by asking her to be disobedient. He's like the neighborhood bully who tells your child, "Go ahead, run into the street. All the big kids do it. You want to be a big kid, don't you? What are you, a baby? Do you have to do everything your daddy tells you? He just doesn't want you to have any fun, that's all."

Like the serpent, the Sirens of stress sing many refrains:

You can stop bad things from happening if you think about them constantly.

I can give you self-esteem if you do just a little bit more . . . and more . . . and more.

Everyone knows that all that "Be not afraid" stuff is meant to be taken metaphorically. No sophisticated person really believes it. All God really means is that you shouldn't worry too much. Trust me. Really.

People will love you if you just take care of all their problems.

We nod, frown sagely . . . and run our craft onto the rocks.

In much the same way that he brought about the destruction of our protoparents, Satan convinces each one of us that anxiety is a necessary part of our contemporary existence. But the truth is that God wants to enfold us in what Scripture calls "the peace . . . that surpasses all understanding" (Philippians 4:7). God did not make us to be worn down and used up by stress. As Paul says to Timothy, "God did not give us a spirit of cowardice but rather of power and love and self-control" (2 Timothy 1:7). God wants us to go out to the world in joy and gladness, shameless and without fear.

Anxiety vs. Prudence

Humorist Garrison Keillor once said, "Sometimes you have to look reality right in the eye . . . and deny it." If you are experiencing anxiety that paralyzes, immobilizes, or confounds you, then I am going to invite you to look at what you think is reality . . . and deny it. I am going to give you the tools to begin seeing through that dark glass to the new world God is creating for you even as we speak.

You may feel foolish at first. You might feel that you are tempting fate or tempting the Lord. But the Lord's ways are high above our ways, and what seems folly to man is wisdom to God—just look at the cross.

But, you may say, what about those times when there is really something to be afraid of? If someone puts a gun to my head, should I "deny reality" and attack my attacker? Should I jump off a cliff because I deny my fear of falling to the ground?

Absolutely not, but I'm glad you asked. Let's take a minute to define our terms. These fears that we just mentioned above, and others like them, are not anxiety. Anxiety is the fear of that which we cannot control and which cannot physically or morally harm us.

To be afraid of something that is beyond our ability to control is foolish. What good will it do? Will worrying about the end of my life postpone my death one minute? Of course not. Is such worry the best way to spend myself when there is so much to do before I die? Likewise, what good does it do to waste time worrying about things that don't cause me physical or moral harm?

There is an aphorism that states, "That which does not kill me makes me stronger." Amen. Why should I fear the nurturing of my strength? No, it is not pleasant to be tested in fire, but metal always needs to be tempered with heat. What better way to test my mettle than through the heat of conflict, growth, and change?

So, if anxiety is the fear that comes from worrying about things that are beyond my control or things that cannot harm me physically or morally, what should I call the fears that overtake me when my physical or moral health is threatened? Ah, that is Prudence. The Siren Anxiety masqueraded as Prudence, but this is the genuine article: fear that prevents me from acting in a way that is contrary to my physical or moral health. Prudence stops me from walking into a dark alley at midnight. Prudence stops me from robbing the bank when it is time to pay bills. Prudence stops me from getting too close to the literal or metaphorical fire.

Thinking about Feeling

Anxiety isn't the only Siren out there luring us to the rocks. My counseling practice is full of well-meaning individuals whose lives are being wrecked because what they think is virtue is actually its perversion. They have been seduced by the Sirens to believe, for example, that what is actually vengeance is justice, what is scrupulosity is temperance, what is pride is fortitude, what is hedonism is joy.

The funny thing is that these pairs of qualities can feel very much the same. Justice and vengeance can both *feel* angry. Temperance and scrupulosity both *feel* cautious, and prudence and anxiety both *feel* fearful, often strongly so. Granted, if we really stopped to experience these feelings side-by-side, we would see that there is an important qualitative difference, but most of us aren't emotionally savvy enough to pick up on it. God gave us our emotions as a kind of early-alert system that calls us to activate virtue. Satan seeks to use our emotions to convince us to activate a virtue's opposing vice.

And this leads us to the next question: "How can I tell the difference between a false emotion and a true one?" The answer is as simple as it is provocative. We need to learn to hear the "song" that is causing the emotional reaction in the first place.

I often ask my clients, "How does the mind create an emotion?" Usually people respond with some version of "Well, something happens to me and then I feel something about it." In other words, most people seem to believe that emotions have a stimulus-response quality to them. "My experience X leads automatically to emotion Y."

In reality, the process unfolds like this: I experience something, then I make an automatic interpretation about that thing, and finally, that interpretation throws the chemical switches that create my emotional response. In other words, "I experience X, which leads me to think Y, which causes emotion Z."

Imagine that you are at the mall. While you are there, you see a friend. You wave at him. He doesn't wave back. Those are the facts, and these facts represent all you know about the interaction. Depending on how your brain interprets these events, you could have several possible emotional reactions. If the automatic interpretation that pops into your head is "I guess he didn't see me," you will feel nonchalant about your encounter with your friend. But what if your mind says, "That jerk! What? Is he too good to be seen with me in public?" Then you are going to feel indignant. Or what if you experience the same situation, and this time the thought that pops into your head is "I wonder what I did to make him so angry that he would ignore me that way?" This time you will feel guilty, even though you have no idea what you might have done wrong, and there is absolutely no indication that you did anything at all.

Curiously, in each of these scenarios, the only thing that is different is the automatic thought that pops into your head telling you how to interpret your experience and what to feel about it. Because our thoughts play such a significant role in determining our emotional state, it is critically important to learn what those thoughts are and to determine if they are true or false.

True-False Test

Once we know what thoughts are triggering our emotional reactions, we need an objective standard to tell us whether our automatic interpretations are true or false. Jesus says, "I am the way and the truth and the life" (John 14:6). As this Scripture indicates, if something is true, it comes from God; therefore, this thing should lead to greater clarity about the way we should go and a fuller experience of life once we get there.

In other words, we know that a thought or feeling is true (healthy, productive, rational) if acting on that thought or feeling would lead us to experience a greater degree of hope, confidence, competence, intimacy, security, peace, strength, and so on, even in the face of problems.

On the other hand, we know a thought or feeling is false (not of God, who is "the way and the truth and the life") if acting on that thought or feeling would lead to hopelessness, confusion, doubt, anxiety, despair, estrangement, insecurity, ignorance, or incompetence, none of which come from God.

In a sense, since none of these qualities comes from God, one could argue that to act on false thoughts and feelings is to allow ourselves to become unwitting participants in Satan's plan of destruction for our lives and relationships. Granted, when we do this we may not be sinning, since we may lack the full knowledge and will necessary to commit sin, but that does not mean that we cannot be used as pawns in Satan's destructive game. Looking at our experience in this light, suddenly we see that each of us has not just a psychological but a moral imperative to get our thinking and emotional life in order.

Let me give you an example. Imagine that I am irritated with you because you forgot to do something I asked. Generally speaking, you are a responsible and considerate person, but this time you dropped the ball, and I am angry.

Now imagine that the unspoken automatic thought going through my head is, "What a jerk! I can't rely on her/him to do anything. (S)he is so irresponsible. Once again, everything falls to me."

Is this automatic thought true or false?

It is false. Why? Because while it is true that you have disappointed me, this automatic thought does not lead me to any practical, hopeful action that would resolve the problem. In fact, the feelings that result from this automatic thought are resentment, estrangement, and despair, none of which come from God. Therefore, while the problem is true, my reaction is false.

Let's try again with the same example. This time, the automatic response that pops into my head is, "This is really upsetting. I wonder why (s)he did that. I think I'll go and ask her/him what happened and see if (s)he can still take care of that for me." Is this thought true or false?

It is true, because it clarifies a productive course of action in the face of my confusion and disappointment. If I act on this automatic thought, I will feel hopeful and proactive. My action may lead to greater intimacy with you when you see that I am being firm but giving you the benefit of the doubt. All of these feelings and fruits do come from God; therefore, this is a true (healthy, respectful, and productive) response.

Once I know what thoughts are going through my head, I can do this simple true-false test to evaluate whether my automatic thoughts are the voice of God leading me out of despair and frustration or the song of a Siren leading me into deeper confusion, hopelessness, and isolation.

Top Ten Types of Faulty Thinking

In addition to the true-false test, other tips can clarify whether an automatic thought (and the resulting emotional reaction) is true or false. Psychiatrists Aaron Beck and David Burns pioneered a breakthrough approach to psychotherapy called cognitive therapy. They suggest that when people are exhibiting emotional problems, their automatic thoughts tend to fall into one or several of ten major categories of cognitive distortions, or faulty thinking patterns. Each of the cognitive distortions represents a lie that we tell ourselves about our circumstances. The degree to which we believe and act on these lies tends to be directly related to how miserable, anxiety ridden, or ineffective we become in the face of problems and conflict.

Each of these cognitive distortions has a grain of truth in it, but it is a twisted truth that causes us to act in false (unhealthy, unproductive) rather than true (healthy, productive) ways. While there are a few others not included on this list, the following represent the ten most common cognitive distortions:

1. Mind reading

I don't think he really loves me. He says he does, and he does nice things for me, but I think it's just because he has to for the kids' sake. He's a very dutiful person. He tells me I'm crazy, and maybe I am, but I think I know him better than he thinks I do.

Mind reading is the cognitive distortion that has one constantly trying to divine what other people are thinking. We say inwardly, "I know what you are thinking better than you do. In fact, even if you tell me what you are thinking, I know what you were *really* thinking, and chances are, it was something negative about me!"

2. Filtering

I can't enjoy anything. Why can't things be just right once in a while? Why does there have to be some little thing that screws it all up?

Filtering is the distortion that occurs when we strain out part of our experience and only respond to that part instead of the whole. We can engage in either positive filtering ("I know he beats me, but he gave me flowers back in 1967, so I know deep down he's really a great guy") or negative filtering ("Even though it looked like the party went perfectly, it was ruined for me because I could not find my favorite punch bowl"). If we never take in the whole picture, we can never find a healthy response to our circumstances.

3. Magnification

I am just so overwhelmed! I have so much to do. Every time I think about starting I feel sick. I don't know how I'm ever going to get it all done!

Imagine standing in the middle of the railroad tracks. A train is bearing down on you, and all you can think is, "How am I ever going to lift this train before it crushes me?" Never mind that if you stepped five paces to the left or right you would be just fine.

Magnification causes us to feel that our problems are so big there is nothing to do but become paralyzed by them. We forget that no matter how big our problems are, God always obliges us to act, even in some small way, trusting that he can multiply our efforts in the same way he multiplied the loaves and the fish.

4. Catastrophizing

The other day my boss told me she wanted to see me later. I spent the whole day worried about that meeting. Did I do something wrong? Was she going to fire me? What if she was upset with me for something? I don't need this stress.

Catastrophizing is a huge contributor to anxiety. I catastrophize when I engage in "what if" scenarios. For example, I watch the disease-of-the-week movie on TV and suddenly become consumed with worry about contracting the disease. Or my spouse and kids are five minutes late coming home, and I automatically think they have died in a fiery explosion. Yes, these things could happen, but in all likelihood they are not happening right now. There are other, likelier explanations for that twinge in my arm or my family's delayed return. I need to explore these more innocent possibilities first before I begin jumping to wild conclusions.

Catastrophic thoughts like these represent Satan's way of causing us to spend all of our energy on imaginary problems so that we don't have the strength to deal with the real problems in our lives. When we catastrophize, we need to remember Jesus' injunction: "Do not worry about tomorrow; tomorrow will take care of itself" (Matthew 6:34).

5. Emotional reasoning

I don't know. One minute my feelings are telling me to leave him. The next minute I can't live without him. I feel so conflicted. On the face of it, everything looks fine. The relationship is OK, I guess. I just don't feel happy, and I don't know why.

Emotional reasoning occurs when we believe that what we *feel* is true must *be* true.

I feel like the sky is falling, that you are attacking me, that everyone hates me; therefore, it must be true. Never mind that the sky is still in the heavens, that I simply misunderstood your intention, and that most people find me quite agreeable. What my emotions say goes.

Of course, this causes me to feel constantly confused and lost, as my feelings change radically from one day (or one minute) to the next. At worst, this is Satan's way of getting me to make stupid and destructive choices with great conviction ("I just feel this is what I have to do, that's all"). At best, it is his way of keeping me paralyzed ("I don't know what to do; my feelings keep changing").

People engaged in emotional reasoning need to stop concentrating on emotions and instead ask, "What is objectively true (healthy and productive)? What is objectively, morally right?" They then need to do what is true and right regardless of what their feelings tell them.

6. Polarized thinking

I feel so paralyzed whenever I try something new. I put so much pressure on myself to get it right the first time, because otherwise, I'll feel like such a total failure.

When we engage in polarized thinking, the world is perceived in black-and-white terms; there is no in-between.

"You are either for me or against me."

"If I can't be perfect the first time, I might as well not try because I am a failure."

"Sometimes I think I love you, and then I think I hate you!"

With polarized thinking, we can never make a decision or act decisively because we can never decide which of the two poles is "correct."

In truth, neither pole alone is correct. We can only arrive at the truth by seeking the middle way between those poles. For example:

"We disagree, but how can we work together to make a plan that meets both of our needs?"

"I may not be perfect the first time, but I will improve with time and practice."

"I love you, but we have some problems that we need to work out."

7. Fallacy of internal control

I just can't say no to anybody. I feel so guilty disappointing people. I like to be helpful, but I feel as though people are taking advantage of me. They just expect me to clean up their messes and, of course, I do.

When I employ the internal-control fallacy, I feel it's my job to make sure that everything around me is perfectly peaceful and everyone around me is perfectly happy. I can never say no, even to unreasonable requests, because I might disappoint someone, and heaven forbid I ever express my true wants and needs in case I ruffle someone else's feathers.

This cognitive distortion makes me feel as if I am the world's big brother and causes anxiety by forcing me to pretend I don't have any needs of my own. Eventually, I will short out. Panic attacks are the common fruit of this distortion. Satan makes us think it is Christian charity, but in reality it is codependency, the need to avoid conflict at all costs and clean up everyone else's mess even when it is not one's moral or psychological responsibility to do so.

8. Personalizing

I was sitting in the meeting the other day and thinking that all these other people are so much more qualified than me. Then I saw Sheila have that look on her face. She probably thinks I'm incompetent.

Personalization manifests itself in several ways. One way is that we think everything that others do is some kind of reaction to us. If you walk into the room with a scowl on your face, I think it is because you are angry with me. If I am in a restaurant and I hear people laughing in the booth behind me, I worry that they are snickering about me.

Personalizing makes us hypersensitive to both perceived and actual criticism. It also causes us to worry about how we measure up to others. "Am I as successful/attractive/intelligent/active as so-and-so? If not, then I must be worthless."

9. The "should's"

My wife tells me that I am too hard on other people, constantly criticizing them. But she doesn't know that I am even harder on myself. I feel so guilty all the time. I constantly worry whether I said or did the right thing. I don't want to offend anybody, or God, for that matter, but I never feel that I can be good enough.

This cognitive distortion causes us to hold legalistic, rigid standards and become paralyzed by anxious guilt or intense anger whenever we, or someone else, does not live up to them. This is not to say that there are not objective standards of behavior or morality, merely that people are not always perfect examples of these standards. We need to cope firmly but charitably with these flaws, not come at them with a whip and a chair. The "should"s represent Satan's way of turning temperance into scrupulosity as we become anxiously obsessed with our own conduct and that of others.

10. The fallacy of change

I get so worked up with my husband. I ask him to do things for me, and he promises the moon but never gets around to anything. I end up pushing and pushing and being a total nag, which we both hate, but I don't know what else to do. I tell him how much his neglect hurts me. I discuss, cajole, complain, ask. He just doesn't seem to get it. And the more I look around at the stuff that needs to be done, the more anxious I get.

The fallacy of change is the song the stress Siren sings to get us to believe that (a) our happiness depends on our ability to get others to change and (b) when they won't change, it's because we're not pushing them hard enough.

While it is a seductive logic, the problem with this thinking is twofold. First, while we might be happier if certain people accommodated us (and perhaps it could be argued that by all rights they should accommodate us), we still have an obligation to find a way to meet our needs even if they don't want to help. In the example above, that might mean the wife will either do the jobs herself or hire them out—with or without her husband's consent.

Second, the more we push others, the more entrenched they become. It is a simple fact of life that if others don't do something when you ask them politely the first or second time, they probably won't do it at all no matter how much you push. Or, if you finally drag them there and make them do whatever it is against their will, you won't appreciate their effort anyway because of all the emotional energy you had to expend.

The more we try to get people to change to suit us, the less they change. And the more anxious we become as we try to control something that is completely beyond our ability to control: the free will of another human being.

Doing Something about It

Let's review what we have learned so far in this chapter.

- It is not events that cause our feelings but our automatic thoughts about or interpretations of those events.
- We must learn to first recognize what automatic thoughts are causing our emotional reactions and then ask whether these thoughts are true or false.
- A true thought is one that leads to hopeful, competent, intimate, respectful, and efficient solutions to the problems we encounter. True thoughts allow us to see the light of Christ shining through the problem situation, drawing us toward greater strength. By contrast, false thoughts lead to a greater experience of hopelessness, despair, anxiety, estrangement, and confusion in the face of a problem. To act on these thoughts is to become unwitting participants in Evil's plan of destruction for our lives and relationships.
- If we determine that an automatic thought is false, it can be helpful to know which of the ten categories of falsehood is being used against us, so we can resist this psychological and spiritual attack.

That's a lot of interesting information, you may be thinking, but exactly how do we exorcise the distorted thoughts from our minds?

I'd like to suggest a specific, three-part journaling exercise to be used any time you are feeling overwhelmed by false automatic thoughts and emotions.

First, you vent the false thoughts. You can't heal a wound until you've cleaned out the infection, and while it is not a pretty metaphor, it is accurate to say that writing down these false thoughts is akin to cleaning out the mental pus that flows from an emotional wound. It is important that you don't just describe what happened. Instead, you might write one simple, declarative sentence about it: "My friend said X" or "My husband did Y." Then spend the rest of the paragraph answering a question about that statement: "What does it mean to me that my friend said X?" or "What does it mean that my husband did Y?"

For example, let's say that one day you receive an unexpected bill in the mail. You gasp in horror and begin to feel the panic hitting you in the chest. Instead of getting hysterical, though, you get out a piece of paper and you write.

> *My HMO denied the hospital bill for Jeremy's broken leg, and I am on the hook for $800! I don't know where I am going to get the money. If things keep going like this, we are going to end up on the street! Why would God do this to us? Sometimes it seems like everything happens to me. I can never cut a break. I don't know what I am going to do.*

After you have vented your spleen, take a minute to reread what you just wrote, as if it were a letter from a friend. Imagine that your friend, not you, is the one thinking and feeling these things. It is your job to (1) help your friend sort out the true and false thoughts and (2) suggest some practical and true tips for addressing the problem at hand. Go through your "friend's" letter line by line, inserting your editorial comments.

My HMO denied the hospital bill for Jeremy's broken leg, and I am on the hook for $800! (True: statement of fact) *I don't know where I am going to get the money.* (True: statement of fact) *If things keep going like this, we are going to end up on the street!* (False: Catastrophizing, magnification. Your family has at least a little way to go before ending up on the street.) *Why would God do this to us?* (False: Personalizing, emotional reasoning. Even though it may feel as if God is moving heaven and earth just to pick on you, it isn't so. How narcissistic is that?) *Sometimes it seems like everything happens to me.* (False: Personalizing, emotional reasoning. Again, everything is not about you). *I can never cut a break.* (False: Filtering. Remember the time when X did go your way and you couldn't stop thanking God?) *I don't know what I am going to do.* (True: statement of fact)

Now that you have sorted out the true and false statements in your emotional rant, take what is true and write a response. Emphasize practical possibilities that increase the chances that you will become more hopeful, competent, peaceful, joyful, and effective, even in the face of this very real concern.

Dear Friend,

I know you just got a bill you weren't expecting, and you are scared. But be careful not to make the situation worse through faulty thinking. The truth is hard enough.

Even though this is a financial setback, you are not going to end up on the street. I know things are tight, but you have robbed Peter to pay Paul before and somehow managed. Remember the time your car broke down and God gave you a gift through your aunt to cover some of the cost? Don't forget to bring this to the

Lord. He expects you to trust that he can multiply your resources too. Likewise, everything bad doesn't always happen to you, even though you may feel right now that it does. Remember when you wanted that promotion and it came through? You couldn't stop thanking God then. Now, let's try to be practical.

As soon as you are finished reading this, talk to the insurance company and appeal the decision. Call the billing office at the hospital and tell them you are appealing it. If you need to pay something, pay the absolute minimum until you can resolve this. Take it one step at a time. If the insurance company does deny your appeal, deal with that problem then and work out payment. Hospitals will usually take as little as $20 a month if they have to, and they're just going to have to. But don't get ahead of yourself. Let the problems you have right now be enough, get more info, and handle one piece at a time.

The stress Sirens are working overtime on this one. Don't let them win.

A few tips for making this journaling exercise effective:

1. **Keep it practical.** Avoid platitudes like "Don't worry. You're going to be OK. God won't give you any more than you can handle." All of these statements may be true, but they lack the weight needed to be any real help to you or anyone else.

2. **Don't give yourself a sappy pep talk; keep it focused on what you need to do.** This response is supposed to orient you to useful, hopeful, effective *action*. If you can't figure out what to do, make that your main mental occupation, not worrying. Ask advice, think, and write down all the

possibilities you can imagine (even the unrealistic ones) as a way of jump-starting your creativity. Put all of your energy into finding solutions, not into nursing your stress.

3. **If you make any positive, supportive statements, give evidence for them** (like the promotion and the gift from the aunt, in the example above). Never preach something to yourself that sounds like a platitude without backing it up with actual experience.

4. **Bring God into the picture, but don't whine to him to do all the work.** Ask him primarily for the grace and wisdom you need to effect a change. Be open to his prompting. As the saying goes, "Pray like it's all up to God; work like it's all up to you." Both are necessary for true change to occur.

3

Spiritual Tools for Overcoming Anxiety

People often ask, "Isn't anxiety just the result of a chemical imbalance?" While it is true that there are neurological and biochemical factors to take into account, it's not quite as simple as saying, "My brain is wired to be anxious; therefore, I must be anxious unless some pill can make me better." Even when medication is indicated, studies show that antianxiety medications reduce only about 30 percent of the symptoms a patient is experiencing. In other words, in many cases, even the best anxiety medications that have the most powerful effect on brain chemistry can still leave you with up to a whopping 70 percent of the anxiety to cope with on your own.

This would be very distressing if we didn't have other tools available to us. As we saw in the last chapter, as we become more conscious of our thoughts (by using cognitive exercises like the journaling technique described, for example), we can change our thinking patterns. This, in turn, can actually change our brain physiology, but a discussion of this is beyond the scope of this book. For more information on the neurological effects of cognitive therapy, I recommend Dr. Jeffrey Schwartz's excellent book *Brain Lock.*

In this chapter, we want to address these questions: Is there a spiritual component to anxiety? What spiritual tools can we use in our struggle to find peace in the middle of the storm?

It is difficult to study the direct effects of spirituality on human beings, but several studies in recent years suggest strong links between one's spirituality and one's health. Variously, researchers report that truly faithful people are happier in their lives, live longer, recover more quickly from treatable illnesses, and endure terminal illness with greater fortitude. Likewise, people of faith have, on average, happier marriages and more satisfying sex lives than their strictly secular counterparts. Spirituality has become so strongly linked to health that as part of their move toward integrated health care, some HMOs are assigning chaplains and spiritual counselors to outpatient health-care centers.

While the connection between a healthy spiritual life and general physical and mental health is becoming more accepted by the general culture, it still leaves several questions unanswered. "Why does spirituality matter?" "How does it matter?"

Though these are infinitely complicated questions, I have always found that the greatest metaphysical mysteries can be digested, if not completely understood, through simple tools. Jesus had his parables, St. Patrick the shamrock, St. Francis the crèche. I'd like to turn to an even simpler source of wisdom, a brief exchange between Pooh and Piglet in A. A. Milne's *The House at Pooh Corner.*

"Pooh?"

"Yes, Piglet?"

"Nothing. I just wanted to be sure of you."

I think this is as good an explanation of how spirituality combats anxiety as any we're likely to find. Here we are, like Piglet, small, helpless, a little pathetic. There is the world, bigger, faster, stronger, and meaner. In such times, it is good to be able to assemble what little courage we have at our disposal and call out.

"God?"

"Yes, Greg?"

"Nothing. I just wanted to be sure of you."

In this simple exchange, we find the answer to our questions. Spirituality helps because it connects us with a force that is bigger than us, a personal God on whom we can rely, of whom we can be sure when we become intimidated by the heffalumps and woozles that plague daily life.

Fear: A Deadly Virus

Before the Fall, God was right there before our eyes. The world was big, but so what? There was God, standing beside us. What did we have to fear? All we had to do was whisper and we could be assured that he would hear. We were "sure of him." But after the Fall our vision became clouded, our ears plugged, our voices choked. God was still present, but we could not see him or be sure he would respond when we cried out or hear him clearly when he did.

And so spirituality became work. Now we relate to God as though we are cloaked in a perpetual fog, relating to the world cautiously, circumspectly, uncertainly. There is so much that we miss, and it is only with great effort that we reconnect with what was to be the most natural of all the parts of ourselves: the ability to call out to the Lord in our weakness, to be confident that God will hear our cry, to trust that his answer, regardless of what it is, will bring peace, joy, and providence.

Now we feel alone. An illusion, of course, but it feels real all the same. And with that sense of aloneness comes anxiety. To our great joy, though, God has been seeking us, calling out to us for millennia. He cries out with joy when one of us responds. Like the shepherd who found his lost sheep, the woman who found her lost coin, the father who finds his prodigal, God does more than most would think reasonable to find what had been lost to him.

I believe that there is no more important spiritual battle a person can fight than the battle against anxiety. Why do you think Jesus spent so much time telling his disciples "Be not afraid" and "Peace be with you"? I would assert that it is because anxiety stands either at the root of all evil or pretty darn close to it. If you look hard enough, almost every sin can be traced back to fear. True, Scripture says that the love of money is the root of all evil. But what causes a person to love money in the first place? The fear of not having enough. Fear stands at the heart of it all.

The thief steals because he is afraid of being without. The child lies because he is afraid of being found out. The young woman sleeps around because she is afraid of being alone. The young man seduces a string of women because he is afraid of commitment. The employee is a workaholic because he is afraid of not measuring up. The mother beats her child because she is afraid of being manipulated. The husband beats his wife because he is afraid of not being in control. The couple divorces because each is afraid of being taken advantage of. The pregnant woman has an abortion because she is afraid she can't raise a child on her own. The depressed person kills himself because he is afraid he can't take it anymore. The list goes on.

We are a fearful people and fear, like a virus, creeps up on us slowly, first choking out our spirits and then snuffing out our lives. Health-science researcher Dr. Nick Cummings has done studies that show that a full 60 percent of visits to the family doctor can be directly attributed to stress-related illnesses (mental and otherwise) and another 20 percent are for illnesses with a significant stress-related component (diabetes, asthma, or heart disease, for example). [2]

Jesus came to conquer not only sin but the fear that lies at the root of sin and disease. After Adam and Eve ate of the tree, the first words Adam spoke to God were, "I was afraid, because I was naked, so I hid myself " (Genesis 3:10). When Jesus conquered that same tree, the first words God spoke to humankind were, "Do not be afraid" (Matthew 28:10). With those words the circle is closed, the damage undone. As Scripture says, "Perfect love drives out fear" (1 John 4:18). Jesus, who is perfect love, desires to drive out the fear from all those who love him and follow him. Will you let him conquer yours?

Coming In from the Cold

MATT TOLD ME THAT HE WAS "COMPLETELY FRIED." The Internet company he worked for was reorganizing, and he was terrified that if he didn't land a major account soon he would be on the unemployment line. In his anxiety, he first isolated himself from God and his family. Then he flogged himself with all the things he "should" be doing.

"I know I should try to pray through this more. And I should try to spend more time with my wife and kids. I just don't know how to make it all happen. I don't have time to pray anymore. Hell, I don't have time to think. And it kills me to admit it, but I don't have time for my family right now either."

---

[2] R. Simon, "Psychotherapy's Soothsayer," *Psychotherapy Networker*, July / August 2001, 34–39.

When I hear stories like Matt's, I remember a bumper sticker I once saw: "I'm so busy, I don't have time to NOT pray." One of the first things anxiety does is turn our priorities upside down. It forces us to be so focused on the need to "fix the problem" that we forget to look around for any tools to work with. We allow ourselves to be cut off from our supports. We alienate ourselves from the God who wants to carry us through this time, the family who wants to love us through our fears, and we forget to use the spiritual and emotional tools that would empower us to succeed in the face of stress.

As Satan whispers thoughts of despair, isolation, and incompetence in our ears, we experience the cold chill of evil traveling through our bodies in the form of anxiety. Imagine being outside on the coldest day of the year. The wind is whipping at your face, drying out your eyes and lips, and burning your nose. You can feel the pain of the damp cold in your fingers and toes, and you marvel at how you can actually feel the chill spreading through your body, as if your veins and arteries were carrying ice water to your extremities. Every part of you feels brittle. You wonder if you will ever get warm again.

The world is a cold place, but God calls us to come in from the cold. He builds a fire for us, makes us a warm drink, and wraps us in the blanket of his perfect love, which casts out fear. Slowly you feel yourself absorbing the warmth. You can feel your body melting one layer at a time until the warmth has taken up residence inside every cell and the chill becomes a distant memory. It is good to be home again.

Nice metaphor, Greg, you may be thinking, *but how do I get a piece of this blanket?* By getting your priorities back in order and reaching for the spiritual tools God has given you to use. By engaging in spiritual exercises like the ones described in the rest of this chapter, it becomes possible to find peace even in the face of extreme pressure.

We will look at the following list, which is by no means

exhaustive: the sacraments, scriptural affirmation, praying the rosary, eucharistic adoration, and sacramentals (things and tokens that remind us of God's loving presence). These are spiritual tools that can help us drive away the chill of anxiety.

Sacred Moments and Sacred Things

In his book, *spirituality@work*, Gregory F. A. Pierce refers to himself as "piety impaired." I think most of us are. I know that I have struggled with piety because it is so often confused with self-righteous pharisaism ("Doing these rituals makes me better than you") and pie-in-the-sky magical thinking ("Lighting these candles and muttering these words will make everything all better"). We who fancy ourselves to be at least part-time intellectuals would like to think that we are above such "silly superstitions."

But there is real power in sacred moments and sacred things. The power is not in the things themselves, but in the God who has chosen to use these things to reveal himself to us. Christianity is a messy, earthy, physical religion. This has always been true, and it has always made people uncomfortable. The Gnostics stripped Christianity of its physicality and made being "Christian" all about pursuing knowledge and nebulous spirituality—not unlike our New Age philosophies today. Even some Christian groups are decidedly uncomfortable with the messiness of Christianity, preferring to emphasize a "spiritual communion" with the Lord instead of sincerely struggling with why the real presence is so important or why God would want to relate to us through anything as earthy as a sacrament, with all its attendant physicality and "mumbo jumbo."

But God created us as *embodied* creatures. Our bodies give us uniqueness and dignity in God's created order. As we profess in both the Apostles' and Nicene Creeds, Christians believe that not only will our spirits rise, our bodies will as well. Our physical being is important to God, and he ministers to our bodies as well as our spirits through physical things. Let's take a look at some of the sacred things God uses to nurture our spirits.

There is no more profound example of God ministering to our souls through physical means than the sacraments. If you know how to use them, they can be an infinite source of comfort for the person suffering from all sorts of anxiety and stress. The three sacraments that help us most in overcoming anxiety are the Eucharist, confession, and anointing of the sick. Let's take a brief look at ways each can help us overcome our fears and anxieties.

The Eucharist

PAUL IS A THIRTY-EIGHT-YEAR-OLD ATTORNEY AND LIFELONG CATHOLIC. He was experiencing a great deal of anxiety related to both work pressures and his marriage. During that time, one of his friends, an evangelical Protestant, invited him to a service at his church. Paul went, he said, "partly out of friendship and partly out of curiosity." He described an experience that led him to a deeper appreciation of his own faith.

"Toward the end of the service, the pastor gave something he called an altar call. He invited those who didn't know Jesus in a personal way to come forward and say publicly that they wanted to love the Lord with all their heart and live a Christian life. I'd never really seen anything like that, and even though I didn't feel the need to go up, it touched me in some way.

"Afterward, it occurred to me that Catholics have a kind of altar call, too, in the Eucharist. Each time we come forward, we receive Jesus as our personal Lord and Savior, not just spiritually, but physically. His flesh becomes our flesh, his blood flows through our veins. How much more personal can you get?"

———————

Paul said that this revelation had a profound effect on his level of stress and anxiety. "My friend told me that when he first 'accepted Jesus into his heart,' he was flooded with a 'peace beyond all understanding.' I started thinking that maybe I wasn't giving the Eucharist the credit it deserved.

"I had always heard that the sacraments had real power, but we had to open ourselves up to grace to take full advantage of it. I thought maybe I hadn't been doing that. I guess I'd gotten lazy after all those years of marching up in line out of habit. But the next time was really different. When I accepted his Precious Body, I said: "Jesus, I love you. I need to know your power and love. Help me make this communion with my whole body and heart, and show me what to do."

Nothing happened at first, but when Paul got back to his pew and began to pray, he felt an overwhelming urge to cry. "I couldn't hold it back. I was so embarrassed. Catholics just don't do that, right? Well, I did. And I felt the Lord was really speaking to me. I heard him in my heart, saying, 'Peace. I love you.' "

That was a defining moment for Paul. "I had always believed in the Lord, but it never really occurred to me that the Lord believed in me. I knew, somehow, that I would make it through all that was going on in my life. I had that peace." Though Paul's ongoing experience of the Eucharist is not always so emotional, it has been much more personal and profound since this moment.

We are told that the sacraments have the power to actually cause what they symbolize. As Catholics, we recognize that the Eucharist not only symbolizes that we are flesh-and-blood sons and daughters of God, but it makes it so. When we meditate on the true meaning of the Eucharist, it is impossible to feel alone. It is impossible to feel powerless. And with that power of God coursing through our veins, it is impossible to be truly anxious. We become like St. Paul, who in prison was able to laugh at the possibility of death and deprivation because the Lord was with him. That kind of confidence is a gift to anyone of us who wishes to call on his name and ask him to free us from the prison of our mind and break the bars of the anxiety that hold us captive.

Lord Jesus,

Help me to know the power of your Precious Body and Blood. I need your peace. I need your love. Hold me. Strengthen me. Let me know that I am your little child. Help me to feel the grace of being your own flesh and blood. Help me to know that it is all right that my life is too big and complicated for me to manage. Because that's what my Father is for.

Amen.

Confession

MONICA WAS IN COUNSELING FOR ANXIETY RELATED TO A TRAUMATIC PAST. This anxiety was affecting her present relationship with her husband. Having been deeply wounded by others, she was now afraid to open up to a man she freely admitted was "really God's gift to me. He is a very good man."

We had been counseling for a while and she was improving, but she seemed to need a little extra push to use the exercises and techniques that were helping her reclaim her life and relationship. She wanted to get better, but it was hard work, and sometimes she just didn't have the strength.

In one session, I shared G. K. Chesterton's wry observation that "psychotherapy is confession without absolution." As part of our work, I suggested that she confess her anxiety and her struggle to overcome it in bimonthly confession. She was surprised at first, and a little put off. "I thought you were blaming me for my problems," she later admitted.

I explained that confession gives us the grace to overcome the obstacles to becoming the people God created us to be. Monica was struggling to trust God's mercy and love in her life and to love her husband as she wanted to, and she was having a hard time being faithful to the exercises we were discussing in her treatment. I suggested that it would be useful to bring these struggles before God in a more formal way than she had done and to ask for his forgiveness and help. She had never thought of confession this way before. "I used to go to confession and recite a laundry list of one-word sins. I never thought of it in terms of helping me share the real struggles on my heart."

Monica went to confession that week and, for the first time, experienced the true grace of the sacrament. "I always kind of felt that if I went to confession, it was because I was supposed to. This time I went with a real desire to experience Jesus, and he was really there."

While she knew that confession wasn't "magic," she found that in some inexplicable way, she was able to be more faithful to the work she was doing in her therapy as long as she continued to make use of regular confession. "When I skipped a couple of weeks, it was harder to stay on track. But whenever I went regularly, I was more mindful of doing the things I needed to do. I was less anxious, and healing seemed more possible in some way."

The eminent psychoanalyst Carl Jung used to say that Catholics made much less use of analysis because confession did such a good job of eliminating the neurotic guilt that lies at the heart of emotional distress. Similarly, I find that when a client combines the practical work of therapy with the grace and accountability of confession, progress in treatment is much more rapid. Regardless of the degree of anxiety you experience in your life, I would suggest that you take your troubles to the Lord in this more formal, sacramental way and ask for his help to overcome the lack of trust in his providence, the doubt in his love, or the pride that keeps pushing God out of the driver's seat.

> Lord Jesus,
>
> Forgive me for the doubt, the fear, and the pride that separate me from your gentle love, providence, and peace. Through the sacrament of confession, heal my broken heart, minister to my troubled mind, and soothe my trembling spirit. Help me to experience your love in the sacrament, to feel your forgiving arms wrapped around me, and to hear your voice telling me to go forth in confidence, freed from the grasp of sin.
>
> Amen.

Anointing of the Sick

ETHAN IS A TWENTY-SEVEN-YEAR-OLD GRAPHIC DESIGNER who was coping with anxiety accompanied by moderate panic attacks. When these attacks would come, as often as two or three times a week, he would experience shortness of breath, tightness and pain in his chest, and sometimes stomach troubles. On one occasion, the chest pain was so bad that he went to the ER of the local hospital. After extensive medical testing and a thorough history pointed not to medical but to social and emotional factors as the most likely source of his anxiety, he was referred to counseling.

Ethan was in therapy for about six weeks and was making fair progress when he came to our session with a look on his face that said he definitely had something to discuss. He explained that he had asked his pastor to administer the anointing of the sick that past week and had received a powerful connection to God's love through the experience.

"I always thought of anointing as last rites, but there was this insert in our bulletin that explained what the sacrament was really supposed to be about. I never knew it, but apparently it's supposed to be about asking the Lord to heal the body, mind, and spirit. The sacrament puts the suffering person in the presence of God and asks for either healing or for the grace to bear the illness better."

Ethan felt that he needed healing, so he asked his pastor if his problems were appropriate for anointing. The pastor offered him the sacrament on the spot. Ethan was touched, both by the offer and the experience.

"It was wonderful to feel ministered to by the church. I felt so alone and ashamed before, like I must be weak or stupid to feel the way I do. But through the sacrament I was able to feel that Jesus cared not only for the big problems in the world but for my problems, too."

Ethan drew a great deal of comfort from the ritual, the prayer, and the personal contact with his pastor, who told Ethan that if he felt it would be helpful, he would be more than happy to administer the sacrament periodically throughout the course of Ethan's therapy. Again, Ethan was pleasantly surprised.

"I thought that anointing was a one-shot deal. It never occurred to me that I could do it again—and for the same illness. My pastor showed me that the Lord wanted to be beside me every step of the way no matter how long it took for me to get better, although he would pray that the grace of the sacrament would speed my healing even as I continued my therapy."

Ethan underwent the anointing of the sick two more times with his pastor throughout the course of my work with him. Each time he reported feeling spurred on, more able to do the exercises I gave him, and more hopeful that he truly would get better.

In my own experience, the gift of hope is one of the most important results of participating in all of the sacraments. Many people, especially people who have struggled with emotional problems for years, find it difficult to believe that they can really ever get better. Anointing, in particular, challenges this notion. Through it we experience Jesus the Divine Physician, who spurs us on to health.

Hope, as one of the three theological virtues (along with faith and love), is a pure gift from God. Though we can do things to increase our openness to the possibility of hope, we cannot claim hope on our own power. I know plenty of people who wished with all their hearts that they could begin to hope again but could not bring themselves to do it. In such times, it is especially important to seek the Giver of such gifts, and there is no better sacrament through which the suffering Christian can seek hope for healing than through anointing.

God's "Time Machine"

While the examples presented in the previous pages are powerful, I want to emphasize that the relief these good people gained from their participation in the sacraments was not merely a psychological phenomenon. Certainly the rituals are comforting, the prayers are inspiring, and the material accoutrements of the sacraments are intriguing, as they should be. Yet there is real power in the sacraments that extends far beyond the psychological comfort one receives from the external signs and symbols. Because they originate with Christ Jesus himself, the sacraments "effect what they signify."

Jesus Christ did not just come for one time and then leave us all alone. He continues to act in the world today. Through the words of sacred Scripture, we hear his voice clear and strong. Through the sacraments, we experience his saving work; we are witness to Christ's healing, teaching, and sanctifying actions every bit as much today as if we were touching the hem of his garment two thousand years ago (see Luke 8:43–48).

As a child, I used to think about how amazing it would be to have a time machine that allowed me to travel back to the days when Jesus walked the earth. As an adult, I see that I don't need a time machine because, through the sacraments, Jesus Christ melts away the boundaries of time and space and comes to me. When we receive the Blessed Sacrament, we are as good as in that room where Christ gave his disciples his own flesh and blood to eat and drink. He is here with us in this time giving us himself as our food and drink. When we confess our sins, we are telling them not just to "some guy" but to Christ himself, who is actually present in the person of the priest who stands *in persona Christi*. When we receive the anointing of the sick, we are touched by Christ himself, who physically and personally intervenes in our disease.

How is this possible? The only correct answer, of course, is "We don't know." That's why the word *sacrament* means "mystery." But even though we don't understand the mechanism, we do understand that Christ, before ascending to his Father, gave the apostles a special gift of his grace reserved just for them and their spiritual descendents. John 20:22–23 tells us that Jesus breathed on his apostles and said: "Receive the holy Spirit. Whose sins you forgive are forgiven them, and whose sins you retain are retained."

Through the centuries this grace has been passed down from the apostles to the men they chose to succeed them (whom we know today as bishops) all the way down to the pastor of your church. This unbroken apostolic line of grace extending from Jesus Christ through centuries of bishops and priests is what allows your pastor to be the special channel of grace through which Christ continues his own work in the world today.

So, when you encounter the sacraments, you encounter Christ himself, up close and personal. And as Scripture shows us, no one who ever approached the Lord in faith left the experience unchanged. Approach the sacraments in faith, then stand up, walk, and live!

Hearing God in His Word

St. Jerome once said that "ignorance of Scripture is ignorance of Christ." We cannot know how God wants us to respond to our anxiety unless we meditate on and repeat to ourselves the messages found in Scripture.

LANA WAS HAVING TERRIBLE TROUBLES AT WORK. Her company was downsizing, and she was on the list of people to be let go. A widow (she lost her husband to cancer two years before) and the mother of three children, ages six to eleven, she was terrified and at a complete loss for what she would do. Moreover, she was angry with God. "Why does he hate me so much? How much does he think I can really take? I made it through Michael's cancer, but I don't think I can take this now."

———

A lot of days, she heard the words of Job's friends ringing in her ears. "I just wanted to curse God and die." She spent a lot of time yelling at God and crying in his presence. One evening as she was praying, her eyes fell on the concordance of a Bible that she had bought years ago when she attended a parish Bible study. Somehow—she says it must have been God, because it was completely unlike her to do this—she decided to look up words like *fear* and *anxiety* and *power* and *peace* and see what the Bible says about these qualities.

"I found Isaiah 41:10, which says, 'Fear not, I am with you; / be not dismayed; I am your God. / I will strengthen you, and help you, / and uphold you with my right hand of justice.' I kept praying that over and over. Every time I journaled, I reminded myself of that Scripture."

Lana also used her rosary in a unique way. "Every day, I would take five of these encouraging Scriptures and pray them on the Hail Mary beads in the decades of the rosary. I would say each of the five verses ten times, with an Our Father and a Glory Be in between and the Hail Marys at the beginning. It helped me so much."

Lana's faithfulness through this trial was rewarded. "There were so many days I wished I would just die in my sleep. I didn't want to kill myself. I just didn't want to wake up the next day. But I kept praying those Scriptures, and God gave me the courage I needed to get a new résumé together and go to interviews and do what I had to do."

Shortly thereafter, Lana found a job as a florist. Her hobby was dried-flower arranging and, on a lark, she applied for the job. She and the owner hit it off, and she was hired on the spot. "I never would have dreamed of doing this for a living. I just thought I needed a job to pay the bills, but I see that God had better ideas. He wanted me to use my talents, and he used that time to get me to take a risk I wasn't willing to take on my own. I know that praying the way I did caused me to be open to all possibilities, and God used that openness."

I would encourage you to delve into God's word so that you can know his promise of peace for you. To get you started, here are some of Lana's favorite Scriptures.

- **Isaiah 41:10** Fear not, I am with you; / be not dismayed; I am your God. / I will strengthen you, and help you, / and uphold you with my right hand of justice.
- **1 Chronicles 22:13** Be brave and steadfast; do not fear or lose heart.
- **Philippians 4:13** I have the strength for everything through him who empowers me.
- **John 14:27** Peace I leave with you; my peace I give to you. . . . Do not let your hearts be troubled or afraid.
- **Hebrews 13:6** Thus we may say with confidence: "The Lord is my helper, / [and] I will not be afraid. / What can anyone do to me?"
- **John 16:33** I have told you this so that you might have peace in me. In the world you will have trouble, but take courage, I have conquered the world.
- **Philippians 4:6–7** Have no anxiety at all, but in everything, by prayer and petition, with thanksgiving, make your requests known to God. Then the peace of God that surpasses all understanding will guard your hearts and minds in Christ Jesus.
- **Matthew 10:29, 31** Yet not one of them [sparrows] falls to the ground without your Father's knowledge. So do not be afraid; you are worth more than many sparrows.
- **Luke 12:32** Do not be afraid any longer, little flock, for your Father is pleased to give you the kingdom.
- **Romans 15:13** May the God of hope fill you with all joy and peace in believing, so that you may abound in hope by the power of the holy Spirit.

A Mother's Love

Mary is the mother of Jesus, and Jesus is our brother through baptism, so Catholics honor Mary as our mother, too. Historically, the church has encouraged Christians to ask their mother for her prayers and gentle comfort when we are frightened and feel alienated even from her son, whom she can then lead us to. That's why in the Memorare we pray:

> Remember, O most gracious Virgin Mary,
> that never was it known that anyone who
> fled to your protection,
> implored your help,
> or sought your intercession
> was left unaided.
> Inspired by this confidence, I fly unto you, O Virgin of virgins,
> my Mother.
> To you I come, before you I stand, sinful and sorrowful.
> O Mother of the Word Incarnate, do not despise my petition,
> but in your mercy, hear and answer me.

Everybody needs a mommy, even spiritual children, and God in his goodness has given us a mother who can wrap us in her arms and carry us to Daddy, *Abba,* when we are too afraid or hurt or angry to go ourselves. She is not a goddess or even a goddess figure. She is simply human, like you and me. But because she carried God within her body, she is the human being who was graced with the kind of intimacy with God that we can only dream of.

God united with her DNA to become human. He grew in her womb. He nursed at her breasts. She changed his diaper, stayed up with him when he cried, took him to temple, played with him, and comforted him when he felt alone. As such, she can help us bridge the distance we place between God and ourselves. (True, Jesus is the bridge between humanity and God, but think of Mary as the guide who holds our hand and takes us across the bridge in those times when we are too afraid to cross on our own). Being completely, totally human, but also being completely and totally intimate with God, she knows what it takes to lead us from where we are into God's lap.

The rosary is a powerful invocation against anxiety. When you were a child and afraid, were you still afraid when your mommy cuddled you in her lap, stroked your hair, and told you to just hold her hand and everything would be all right? When you pray the rosary, you fly to your mother. Always glad to see you, she takes you in her arms and holds you. And all of a sudden, your daddy is there too. She has brought you to him. And you have nothing to fear.

In her book *The Seeker's Guide to the Rosary*, jazz singer Liz Kelly writes:

> *To say that my life was not functioning would be a gross understatement. I was depressed, barely able to function in the professional world, and growing further and further isolated. So much repressed anguish was now gushing forth in one long, drawn-out, murky cry that I didn't know what to do. I thought I might be losing my mind. Maybe I was not far from it.*
>
> *That's where rosary meditation finally found me—sinking under the oppressive weight of unaddressed personal wounds that I carried in silence and secrecy. I wanted peace. But God felt unfathomably far away, well out of earshot of my supplications. In despair, I turned to the rosary. In my emotional and spiritual turmoil, I could pray no other way.*
>
> *. . . I was relieved by the rosary's simplicity and uniformity. As a former runner, I found the repetition of prayers comforting.*

Something in that simple repetition lent itself to transcendence.
It was like the runner's high I'd felt during long, hard workouts,
when my brain could rest and my body could absorb itself in its
strenuous task. The rosary silenced the craziness in my head and
heart.

. . . Little did I know that those beads held transforming
power. Little did I know that I was reaching out to the ultimate
human intercessor. Mary, like any devoted prayer partner,
would stand in the gap that loomed between God and me.

The rosary was Liz's lifeline through all the hard work of emotional
and spiritual healing. Mary led Liz to her son, Jesus, and comforted
Liz in her arms and helped to wipe the dirt off of her face and clean
her up so that Liz, who felt too dirty, too broken to stand in Christ's
presence, could stand there confidently.

Your mom wants to help you too. Why don't you ask her? Write
a letter to Mary telling her your troubles, explaining why you aren't
sure God will really hear you, and asking her to hold you and pray
with you so you don't have to be alone in the dark.

Spending Recess with God

When I was a child, I was teased a lot. I was also beaten up and
ostracized through most of my grade school and middle school
career. I was too religious, too fat, and too sensitive. Unlike the
other kids who took teasing in stride, I took it seriously. As an only
child for most of my childhood (my sister didn't come along until
I was sixteen), I grew up around adults—people who didn't say
things unless they meant them. When the kids said the cruel things
they just say without thinking, I thought they meant them, and I

cried, which caused them to tease me more. I was an easy mark, usually too gentle to fight back, and when I got the courage, I was too clumsy to do anything but make a bigger fool out of myself.

I remember times when I would feel so sad and alone that I would wonder about dying and wish that I could. I remember once, it must have been in sixth grade, thinking about hanging myself. Even though I wasn't terribly serious, I was serious enough, and I wondered what it would be like, if it would hurt, if I could actually do it if I had to. One day during this very dark time I was taking my dog for a walk. I slowly started pulling the leash up higher and higher until she started gagging. I stopped immediately because I saw how painful it was for her. I loved her and I didn't want to hurt her. And I decided that hurting myself probably wasn't that hot an idea either.

Across the playground from my Catholic school was a church. Almost every recess, I used to sneak away and hide out there. Sometimes I would cry. Sometimes I would just read. Nothing more spiritual than the Hardy Boys, mind you, but I was there, and I felt God's presence.

Some days, the Blessed Sacrament would be exposed for adoration, sometimes the Precious Body was simply in the tabernacle, but I would see God on the altar or imagine him in the tabernacle, and talk to him—aloud, if there wasn't anyone else in the church. I would share with him, cry and yell at him, and even play with him, almost every day from third to eighth grade. Over those many years, God and I formed a very intimate friendship.

I survived childhood for two reasons: (1) My parents loved me, and I knew it, and (2) God loved me, and I knew it. I knew God loved me because when I would stare into his face in the Most Holy Sacrament of the Altar, I would see him looking back at me in love. There was no pain too great, no fear too big that he wouldn't, couldn't love me through it.

I didn't say any special prayers. I didn't have any special knowledge. I was nine, for heaven's sake. I just sat there, and God reached out to me because I was putting in the time. It didn't matter that my motivation wasn't entirely pure. God accepted my presence, and he reached out to me and loved me where I was, for who I was.

I am crying as I write this. Not because I am remembering the pain of that time; that has long passed. Rather, I am crying because I am remembering the love I felt in his presence. I am remembering the love that kept me alive when my teachers, the principal, or even my loving parents couldn't make the kids stop hating me.

You may be surprised to know that, looking back, I am grateful for that time in my life, as painful as it was. I am grateful not only because it helped me become who I am today, but because even when I have suffered crushing defeat or intense fear in my adulthood, I have all those years of God staring me in the face to fall back on. Then, I go and visit him again and tell him I love him. And somehow, that lessens the fear I feel.

When your burdens are too heavy and fear is clouding your vision, go and sit in his presence and look at him. He will do the rest. He will give you the strength to, as Scripture says, "conquer overwhelmingly" (Romans 8:37).

Instruments of Grace

The last of the spiritual tools we're examining here is sacramentals.

"Sacra-which?" you say.

Well, *sacrament* comes from the Latin *sacramentum*, which was the early Christian rendering of the Greek word "mystery." So a sacramental is, literally, "something relating to a mystery." Clear as mud, right?

Simply put, a sacramental is anything that reminds us of the greatest mystery in the world: that God is with us, that he loves us, and that every day he is struggling, suffering, and celebrating right beside us.

MOIRA WEARS A SCAPULAR, A SMALL CLOTH MEDALLION worn close to her heart, that reminds her to keep the Lord and his mother close at all times. "When I start to feel anxious, I press it to my chest and ask Jesus to hold me in his arms. It reminds me that I'm not alone."

BILL HAS SEVERAL ICONS HANGING IN HIS HOME that hold a deep personal meaning for him. "My family is from Eastern Europe, and icons are the art of the Eastern Church. When I feel lost, I look at those images and I think how it was Jesus who brought my family safely here all the way from the old country. That same Jesus helped my great-grandfather find a wife and a home and work here when he had nothing and no one and nowhere to keep them. That same Jesus has been with my family for generations, and that same Jesus is going to help me through whatever struggles I'm facing."

JENNIFER KEEPS HOLY WATER IN HER HOME as a personal reminder to let God's grace rain down on her and her family. Each night she sprinkles it on her children as a reminder of their baptism and of God's presence with them. Each day, she uses it to bless herself with the sign of the cross, "so I can remember that Jesus is my protection and shield."

DEREK WEARS A MEDAL OF ST. MICHAEL THE ARCHANGEL to remind himself of God's power and of the company of angels protecting him all day long. "St. Michael is a powerful image for me. All the drawings show him keeping

Satan at bay at the point of his lance. I ask God to give me that same strength to keep evil and harm out of my thoughts and choices."

———————

Each one of these simple, physical things is a sacramental of one sort or another. That is, they are physical instruments of God's grace. When we use them, we wrap ourselves in a blanket of grace that keeps us warm when the cold winds of stress blow hard against us. In a sense, they represent both the light spiritual nourishment that keeps us going throughout the day and the spiritual first aid that patches us up when we slip.

Sacramentals not only serve as reminders but also convey a real grace, since they are usually blessed objects that hold within them the power of Christ's touch passed on to those objects by the priest who blessed them. But other simple things, though they do not carry this special sacramental grace, can also be used by God to minister to us. In a loose sense of the word, these things could be considered modern-day sacramentals.

JAMES LOVES CHRISTIAN MUSIC. "Christian music ministers to my heart. When I listen to it, I feel like I am being wrapped up in the Lord, like he's all around me. I hear him in my ears. I feel his rhythm in my body. I can't get too lost when I have that CD blaring."

———————

ALEXIS KEEPS A PRAYER JOURNAL in which she writes the things for which she is grateful as well as her petitions and insights. "When I'm feeling stressed out, I read back through all the fears God saw me through and the blessings I've received, and I reconnect with him again. It keeps me grounded when my head is swimming."

———————

What helps you feel close to God? Make a list of all of the physical things that you could use to help keep you spiritually grounded. Likewise, ask the people closest to you what they use to keep God close. Jot these things down too, and see what effect they have for you. Look for the things that keep you connected to the divine and keep these things close at all times. They are your little reminders that God wants to give you his infinite power and love. And if the Lord is for you, who can be against you?

What things remind you of God's presence in your life? How can you use these things, and things like them, to a greater degree in order to amplify your experience of God's grace and anxiety-relieving power?

Fueled by Grace

In this chapter we examined many things and heard from many people about the spiritual tools that help them find the grace to make their lives more anxiety-proof. I believe the tools outlined in this chapter are essential for anyone seeking inner peace. Even the most powerful psychological techniques are rendered at least ten times more powerful when they are fueled by grace.

I used to have a primarily secular counseling practice and worked with a primarily secular group of clients. I was able to do a great deal of very good work with these very motivated individuals, but when God changed the makeup of my practice to consist entirely of Christians, I saw something amazing.

Many of my Christian clients experienced more pathology, faced more troubled marriages, and encountered more challenging family situations than my non-Christian clients ever had to cope with. Even so, the same tools I offered to my non-Christian clients took on new strength when applied by people of grace. Changes occurred in the lives of my Christian clients that I never thought were possible—changes that I helped facilitate, but that deep in my heart I knew were far beyond my meager power to effect.

Marriages that I thought were doomed improved. Children who were hopelessly defiant became children whom any parent would be proud to have. Lives that were broken and scarred by abuse and trauma, the like of which I had not encountered before, were transformed.

These changes did not happen overnight, and in many cases they took an immense amount of work. But by all indications, these changes should not have been possible at all, much less to the degree that they were occurring before my eyes.

I cannot explain these facts, and I will not diminish them by trying. I can only stand in awe of the power of God and invite you to share in the mystery of that power, so that through it all you can remain fearless, confident in your ability to accomplish all things through Christ who strengthens you.

4

Become Who You Are

There is a type of counseling called narrative therapy that proposes a profound concept. Specifically, you must think of the problem you are facing as if it were something outside of you, like a virus, a monster, or a demon—something that has the ability to get inside of you and do damage but is an entirely separate being. Rather than thinking of yourself as "depressed" or "anxious" or "stressed" or "obsessive," you must learn to make the distinction between who you really are and who you are when you are under the influence of depression, anxiety, stress, or obsessive thoughts.

Narrative therapy asks us to examine the stories we tell ourselves and believe are true, but which in reality are just fictions that have been told to us (or that we have told to ourselves) so many times that we believe them to be true.

The fact is that we tell ourselves some interesting fictions about our emotional problems. We identify with them and speak of them as if they are an essential part of who we are. "I am anxious." "I am depressed." "I am obsessive." We say these things with a hopeless shrug. "That's just who I am, that's all."

While these statements seem innocent enough, there is an insidious lie implied by them. If I "just am" that way (anxious, depressive, obsessive, angry, etc.) then there is nothing I can do about it. I just have to suffer, and you just have to accept me, miserable wretch that I am. This story I tell myself about my emotional struggles keeps me trapped, hopeless, stuck.

Isn't it odd that while we tell identity stories about our emotional problems, we don't speak of physical problems in the same manner? We don't say, "I am flu" or "I am high blood pressure." We say, "I *have* the flu." "I *have* high blood pressure." This distinction is more than semantics. When I say that I *have* the flu, the implication is that I can also *not have* the flu. When I say that I have high blood pressure, hidden within that statement is the understanding that I may also overcome this problem. But when I say "I am anxious" or "I am stressed," I imply that it is a hopeless situation. There is nothing I can do about it.

I believe the reason we don't tell ourselves "identity stories" about physical illnesses is that we understand that they come from outside of us. We recognize that since we would function so much better without these physical problems, they must not be an essential part of our makeup. Consequently, we resent these viral intruders and seek treatment to overcome the physical limitation placed on us by the germ or other disease-causing agent. We want to become who we really are, that is, the people we are when we are not under the influence of the disease.

Though we have not trained ourselves to think so, this same logic applies to emotional problems. I function so much better without anxiety, without depression, without obsession, without internal stress; therefore, these qualities must not be natural to me. Rather, they are the result of my mind and soul having been infected with a different kind of pathogen, the false thoughts and cognitive distortions we explored in chapter 2.

What God Has in Mind

MONICA IS A THIRTY-TWO-YEAR-OLD MOTHER OF THREE. "I'm just an anxious person, I guess. I worry about my husband, if he'll come home safe. I especially worry about the kids and whether I'm a good enough mom to them. They're an incredible responsibility. I don't want to screw them up, but I know that my anxiety makes me a perfectionist, which is probably screwing them up, which makes me feel guilty on top of it all. I don't know what to do about it, though. I've always been this way. It's just who I am. I guess it's my cross."

———————

LARRY IS A TWENTY-SEVEN-YEAR-OLD PHYSICAL THERAPIST. A single man who desperately wants to get married, he becomes very anxious around women. "I'm just not a confident person. I go out on a date and I feel like such an idiot. I'm sure the girl is going to think that there is something wrong with me. I'm a pretty nervous person. I don't really think I have anything to offer a woman. At least, not once she gets to really know me."

———————

Clearly, the "identity stories" Monica and Larry are telling themselves are filled with examples of false thoughts as we defined that phrase in chapter 2. We know that the thoughts and stories are false, not because they do not describe a true struggle, but because in the face of that struggle, they cause Monica and Larry to feel hopeless, helpless, confused, despairing, incompetent, estranged, and guilty. Since you will not find any of those qualities, or anything like them, listed among the gifts and fruit of the Holy Spirit, we can reasonably assume that these thoughts do not find their source in the divine. They must be rejected as distractions from becoming the people God wants us to be.

Monica's and Larry's stories would be true, i.e., would lead them to experience feelings of hope, courage, strength, competence, joy, peace, and intimacy even in the face of problems or trials, if they were to say something like this: "I feel anxious a lot of the time, and I have felt that way a good part of my life. But every day, I struggle against that anxiety. I do what I know is healthy and true no matter what my feelings tell me about myself because, right now anyway, I know my feelings aren't leading me to become the person God wants me to be."

Throughout his writings, Pope John Paul II has encouraged us to "become who we are." And who are we really? We are people created by God to function according to our design, to be trusting, loving, functioning, perfected people who operate according to the principles put forth "in the beginning."

When each of us was created in our mother's womb, God had in his mind an image of who he wanted us to become and what mission he wanted us to fulfill. Metaphorically speaking, he encoded that identity and mission into a tiny seed that he planted deep within our soul. Once that seed germinates through an encounter with grace at baptism, it continues to call out to us and make us dissatisfied with anything less than the identity and mission we were created to fulfill. It is the spiritual equivalent of what psychologist Abraham Maslow calls our "actualizing tendency."

That seed is the way God calls us toward greater growth and perfection. That seed, on which is engraved a tiny image of the person we are to one day become, is what God sees when he looks at us. It is that image that we will be confronted with on our passage to the next life. In that moment, we will see what we have become side-by-side with who we really are.

Revealed by Grace

It is a gross mistake, then, to think that what you have become today is who you really are. None of us is who we are . . . yet. The church tells us that we as Christians are called to spend our lives working to become who we are. This is, I believe, what Paul refers to when he says, "Work out your salvation with fear and trembling" (Philippians 2:12). True, we are saved by the passion, death, and resurrection of Jesus Christ, but by cooperating with his grace over a lifetime and becoming who we were created to be as a result of that grace, we "work out [our] salvation," often with a great deal of attendant fear and trembling.

In the theology of St. Thomas Aquinas, there was a saying that "Grace builds on nature." In other words, grace can take the miserable, wretched thing that we are and turn it into something wonderful. But as John Paul II has shown us, there is another way to think about what grace does. The idea of "become who you are" implies that grace does not merely build on our fallen nature but reveals our true nature. Specifically, grace reveals the good, true, beautiful, and divine nature with which we were created, and to which we struggle to claw our way back.

In *Human Development and Human Possibility: Erikson in the Light of Heidegger*, psychologist Richard Knowles demonstrates the phenomenological philosophy that serves as the foundation of Pope John Paul II's view of the human person. In it, he talks about the "fallen self" versus the "authentic self." Regarding this fallen self, Knowles writes:

> *By this term, [Heidegger] means the typical way in which we are occupied by the daily events of life . . . and the way in which this involvement enables us to avoid confronting basic issues. . . . Heidegger calls this mode [of being] inauthentic, meaning that it is precisely in this aspect that we are not ourselves.*

To put it another way, we are so consumed with thoughts of "what shall we eat, what shall we drink, what shall we put on today," not to mention how shall we get done all that we need to do and schlep the kids everywhere they need to go, that we forget that these mere activities do not represent who we really are. They are merely an aspect of what we do.

To get lost in these activities, allowing them to make us forget about God and who he is calling us to become, causes anxiety. It causes anxiety because, if we live our lives this way, then when we imagine ourselves we picture a disfigured creature whom we find, at least, disappointing or, in the extreme, disgusting. When we look in the mirror we see a person who is incapable, ineffective, and hopelessly lost in the overwhelming events of the everyday. But this is not who we really are!

Grace reveals our true, authentic, transcendent self. This is the self who, with God's grace, is more than sufficient to rise above the challenges and petty anxieties of daily living and to use these experiences to become who we really are.

The Authentic Self

So, who are you? To answer this question, I want you to imagine who you would be if you could access all the gifts and fruits of the Holy Spirit at will and use them whenever you needed them to bring clarity and resolution to the trials and challenges of your daily life. What would that be like? That is your authentic self. That is who the church tells you that you really are, who you were created to be, and who, by God's all-powerful grace, you will become once again.

While it is true that, due to our fallenness, we will not achieve the fullness of our perfection in grace until the next life, Christ calls us to begin the pursuit of that perfection now. "So be perfect, just as your heavenly Father is perfect," Jesus says (Matthew 5:48). In this, he tells us to not accept anything less than the best from ourselves. We could never hope to succeed in this struggle on our own, but, as Scripture says, we can do all things through Christ Jesus who strengthens us (see Philippians 4:13). We will aim high, do what we can, and God will fill in the gaps.

Later in this chapter I am going to give you a simple exercise that will help you begin to cooperate with grace to peel away the layers and reveal your authentic self. But first I want to examine some of the virtues that make up that authentic self. As you read through the list, you may be tempted to say, "That's not who I am; I only wish I were more like that." This statement is a lie. Through baptism, each of us is given these virtues in their mustard seed state, as a free and unmerited gift. They represent who we are, at the core, as sons and daughters of the Most High God. We do not claim these virtues on our own, but we have them nevertheless because God in his goodness has given them to each of his children. If you feel that you do not exhibit a particular virtue in your everyday life, it is not because you do not have it. It is merely that you have not watered the seed that has been planted within you. But if you want to allow your authentic self to blossom, it is time to get out the hose.

1. The Theological Virtues

The three theological virtues are gifts God gives us to help us understand his own life and make it possible for his life to be intertwined with our own.

Faith: A gift from God that allows you to be aware of his presence in your life and invites you to want him to become a greater part of your life.

Hope: Confidence that God will never abandon you or forsake you because neither death, nor life, nor any living creature, nor circumstance can come between you and God's love.

Love: Your willingness to work for the good of another, whether or not you "feel" like it. The greatest of all virtues, practicing love empowers you to act as God himself acts.

2. **The Cardinal Virtues**
   From the Latin word for "hinge" (*cardine*), these are the four virtues on which our ability to lead solid, Christian lives hinges.

   Prudence: The practical "know-how" that helps you apply all the Christian virtues to the specific circumstances of your everyday life, helping you avoid things that are harmful to your physical, psychological, or spiritual being and causing you to embrace those things that are good.

   Justice: Your desire to help others achieve all that God wants them to have, your willingness to stand up for what is rightfully yours, and your personal commitment to work for the common good of your family, church, and community.

   Temperance: Your ability to enjoy good things without letting them become a distraction or obsession.

   Courage (also known as *fortitude*): Your willingness to live Christian virtues even when doing so causes you to risk personal discomfort, fear, or rejection or persecution from others. Courage and fortitude represent the drive and desire to become your authentic self, no matter how difficult the journey may be.

3. **The Twelve Fruits of the Holy Spirit**
These qualities especially are the ideals every Christian wants to encourage and nurture in his or her life: charity, joy, peace, patience, kindness, goodness, generosity, gentleness, faithfulness, modesty, self-control, chastity.

4. **Other Virtues of Value**
While the following virtues are not listed among the gifts and fruits of the Spirit, arguably they are no less important to the Christian walk: solidarity (empathy/standing with others in the pursuit of the common good), hospitality, openness, knowledge, creativity, respect, intimacy, obedience, service, attentiveness, wisdom, understanding/compassion, counsel/support, fear of the Lord (joyful awe and respect of God's goodness and power), piety (an acknowledgement of the respect we owe God—and things sacred—throughout our day).

It's There When You Need It

All of the virtues defined above are your inheritance in Christ through baptism. Granted, it takes work to claim them and practice to perfect them, but they are already present within you, and they will be revealed to you as you need them.

This last point is key. Often, people sit around waiting to *feel* courageous or joyful or wise or any of the other virtues God willingly shares with his children before they take actions that could help them overcome the problems in their lives. They say, "I could never do X. I'm not courageous, strong, smart, patient, joyful enough yet. Maybe someday . . ."

These individuals find themselves stuck for life, because this is not how God works. God does not want you to rely on yourself or to think that you are the source of your strength. He wants you to trust him. Therefore, God will not reveal these virtues to you before you need them and call upon him in faith.

That means that courage will not come until you have put yourself in a situation that requires it and you ask God for it. Chances are, you may feel fearful until that moment. Wisdom will not come until you step out in faith and seek it, and chances are you will feel uncertain right up until that moment. Joy will not come until you put yourself in situations where it is required of you, and then you ask God to give it to you. Chances are it will evade you right up until that moment. Then, all at once, there it is.

Not a minute sooner, but not a second too late, you will discover that something you feared you did not have was actually there all the time. Thanks be to God!

Discovering What's Already Inside

ELENA, AGE FORTY-THREE, WAS AN ARTIST. Or at least she wanted to be. She was stuck in a dead-end job with what she called a "dead-end life." She was a very talented painter but was terrified of showing her work to anyone. "What if it stinks? What if I make a fool out of myself? Everybody who ever put a brush to a canvas thinks he is Picasso. What if I'm just as deluded as the rest?"

Over the course of several sessions, I explained to her how to distinguish the difference between her fallen and her authentic self and encouraged her to devise a step-by-step plan that would allow her to overcome her fear, claiming the courage God wanted to give her. Finally, it came to the place where she made an appointment to take her work to a gallery to have it evaluated for its commercial and artistic merit.

"I was terrified. I almost canceled the appointment. And when I got there, I almost didn't go in. But I just kept praying, 'God, give me the courage to do this' over and over, and I kept trusting that God was going to come through, even though I felt sick to my stomach the entire time."

Against her better judgment, Elena kept the appointment with the gallery owner. "It ended up being a very positive meeting. He didn't like everything I showed him, but his comments were very helpful, and I learned a ton. There were even some things that he liked a lot. He told me that if I could develop a few more pieces like those, he might be willing to include me in a show!"

Elena put more energy into her painting. She kept her day job, but she began to see herself more and more as an artist. She took college art classes, worked on her style, and within six months, revisited the gallery. Her meeting was again very positive.

Elena used to think that she was hopeless, a frightened washout whose life was half over and going nowhere. She spent her days worrying about how unfulfilled she was and how hopeless everything seemed, and she spent her nights fearing death, convinced that God would find her wanting when she appeared before him. She was surprised to discover that this pathetic, fallen self was not her true self and that the more she asserted her true self, the more capable, hopeful, confident, trusting, and vibrant she became. Grace revealed her true nature.

It took a great deal of work, but the work did not involve developing virtues and personality traits that she didn't have. It involved showing up for her life and trusting that even through the fear, God would help her discover the strengths and virtues he had planted in her.

"I have never felt more alive," Elena says. "I am becoming who God made me to be, and it was there all the time. This whole thing has given me a new appreciation for who God is, too. I used to think of him as a hands-off God who expected my prayers and loved me from a distance. Now, I see that he loves *me* and that he cares about the dreams in my heart because he created my heart in the first place. He wants me to succeed and will suffer and encourage and celebrate with me all along the road."

She went on to describe an event that marked a major milestone in her spiritual development. "This Advent, when I was in church and heard about 'Emmanuel, God with us,' I really felt like God was *my* Emmanuel for the first time. That he was with *me*. I am so sorry it took me so long to wake up to his generosity, but I am so grateful for him and his love."

Authentic vs. Fallen

I want to lead you through a process that will help you first separate who you are when you are under the influence of anxiety or stress from who you are as your authentic self. Then we will apply this authentic self to the problems you experience in your everyday life.

First, take a piece of paper and divide it into two columns. Over the first column, write "Fallen Self." Over the second column, write "Authentic Self."

Remember, the fallen self is the you that often feels powerless, hopeless, fearful, insecure, confused, and overwhelmed. None of these are virtues that come from God; therefore, they are false. Building your emotional life and actions around such qualities leads to a false and fallen life.

By contrast, the authentic self is apparent in those times when you are proud of your response to others or to difficult situations, those times when you feel that God was with you and you were able to transcend your typical imperfect reactions and made a response that left you feeling capable, confident, grateful, joyful, wise, and even courageous.

In considering the authentic self, don't think of some imaginary self that is capable of walking on water or that glows in the dark from the power and holiness you exude. Rather, think of those times when you were able to be effective, productive, confident, and in control despite internal emotions, people, or situations that sought to discourage you from doing so.

Once you have given yourself several examples (preferably ten

SAMPLE "FALLEN SELF/AUTHENTIC SELF" CHART

Fallen Self	Authentic Self
I got into an argument with my son when I saw that he hadn't cleaned his room yet. →	When I get my children to listen by being firm and listening to them, and letting the consequences do the talking when they are disobedient, instead of arguing.
I just didn't show up for the community meeting after I promised to be there because I was too embarrassed to call and say I couldn't make it. →	When I tell people the truth. Like that time I had to tell my boss that I couldn't make the Saturday morning conference because it was my daughter's birthday.
I wanted to volunteer for that project at work, but I didn't because I was afraid I couldn't do it (even though I knew I probably could). →	When I take risks, like the time I tried out for that play even though I had never done anything like that before.

or more) in each category, review them. I want you to see that instead of just one of you, there are actually two selves, you and your "evil twin"! In other words, there are times when your fallen self is all too present. But there are other times when your authentic self shines out.

This is important because you need to understand that the authentic, true self, the self that is anxiety-resistant, is not some far-off dream. Sometimes your authentic self is right there, and you are able to function as the person you were created to be. This is when you are most "yourself," when you are who you really are. By contrast, in the times when you are acting from the fallen self, you are not who you really are. In those times, you are under the influence of the false-thought "viruses."

The problem is that we have a tendency to move between these two selves almost unconsciously. We tend to think, "Sometimes I have it all together and sometimes I don't, but I have no idea why." The chief reason for this unconscious shift is that it never occurs to most of us that (1) we are truly impaired when we are functioning in our fallen selves (because we think that's just how we are) and (2) there is something we can actually do about this impairment, other than hope by some miracle that it will go away on its own (it rarely, if ever, does).

Having established that your authentic self is not just some far-off, distant wish, I want to expand this exercise in a way that will help you gain greater conscious access to your authentic self so that you can choose to be authentic even in those situations where you currently find yourself struggling.

Take a different piece of paper now and make four columns.

In the first column, "Problem Situations," list situations that cause you to feel powerless, overwhelmed, or anxious. Don't describe your feelings, just stick to the facts of what is happening.

In the second column, "Fallen-Self Reactions," briefly describe the feeling and behavior you demonstrate that makes you feel foolish or not yourself, or at least not your best self.

Incidentally, the reason that this column is called "Fallen-Self Reactions" is that the behavior demonstrated here is often just that, a thoughtless reaction. In other words, it is not a conscious, or a responsible, or a well-thought out response. That is why it is fallen. The key to uncovering your authentic self in these fallen moments is becoming more conscious of your emotions and behavior and consciously directing yourself toward a true and effective course of action.

In column three, "Virtues Needed," ask yourself, "What virtues do I need to uncover in order to be more true, that is, more competent, confident, strong, hopeful, joyful, peaceful, or effective?" The key to success here is finding the balance between two opposite virtues, for example, justice and mercy, patience and persistence, kindness and firmness, generosity and assertiveness.

When we operate in our fallen selves, we tend to express only one virtue at a time. The wife who is being verbally abused by her husband tells herself that she must be patient. The man who is overreacting to a perceived offense justifies it by saying that he is "only doing what is just." The problem is that when a virtue is not balanced by its opposite virtue, it can easily become a vice. If temperance is not governed by prudence, scrupulosity results. If justice is not tempered by mercy it becomes vengeance. If kindness is not flavored with fortitude, it becomes codependency.

Look back at your fallen reactions. Is there some attempt at a virtue there? There may or may not be. If there is, what other virtue do you need to add to make it more balanced and effective?

Identifying the virtues needed to be more effective in any given situation does two things. First, it tells us what to pray for in that moment. Second, it gets our mind working in the direction of an authentic solution, which leads us to the fourth column.

In the final column, we identify our "Authentic-Self Responses." Here we formulate a specific and practical plan that will allow us to script exactly what we must do and say to manifest those virtues we identified in the "Virtues Needed" column. The key to success here is not to be too general. It does no good to say, "I need to be patient." For example, how will I be patient? What will I say? What will I do to express that patience? Without being able to answer these questions, my plan is doomed to fail like all those New Year's resolutions that are also too general to be effective.

The Truth Will Set You Free

Sometimes it is difficult to come up with these authentic solutions. Our minds are so clogged with "thought viruses" and our spirits are

SAMPLE FOUR-COLUMN "CHOOSE TO BE AUTHENTIC" CHART

Problem Situations	Fallen-Self Reactions
My wife gets angry.	I feel frustrated, like "Here we go again," and I ignore her and go into my cave until it's safe to come out again.
My child speaks disrespectfully.	I scream at him and take away privileges, but it doesn't work, and I feel like a terrible mother.
My husband is late getting home.	I feel like I'm not important to him and that he doesn't really love me, so I sulk and pout when he gets home.

so affected by the disease of fallenness that we are sometimes hard-pressed to think of true answers. But there is always an authentic solution. Think hard. Pray harder. If you can't discover it on your own, ask for help. Find a reasonably authentic person (that is, not someone who will tell you only what you want to hear, but someone whose life you admire and who seems to have his or her act together) to encourage you toward what you sincerely believe is an authentic solution.

If you get nothing else from this chapter, I want you to see that you are not doomed to the anxiety that you experience in your life. Your mind may be infected by anxiety, by doubt, by hopelessness, by despair, but you are not, at your core, a person who is anxious, who is doubtful, who is hopeless, who is despairing. Your mission is to work to claim your virtues and pray without ceasing in order to be healed of the infection that clouds your mind and poisons your soul so that your true, authentic self can be revealed and expressed.

Virtues Needed	Authentic-Self Responses
I'm trying to practice self-control by not saying anything, but I need to exercise understanding and assertiveness as well as self-control.	I will tell her that I honestly want to hear what she has to say, but I can only listen if she speaks to me calmly and respectfully.
I'm trying to be firm, but I must add fortitude, wisdom, and discipline to that patience.	I will tell him that he must repeat what he said in a more respectful way. I will not let him off the hook no matter how many times he has to repeat himself until he has used the tone and words I deem appropriate.
I'm not demonstrating any observable virtue. I need to practice assertiveness, understanding, patience, trust, and courage when confronting him.	I will be patient with his explanation, but insist that in the future he call if he is going to be late. If he forgets, I will not pout or complain. I will simply take the children out to dinner and a fun evening so I don't sit around feeling sorry for myself all night. I will be joyful, assertive, and proactive in the face of this slight.

At your most essential core, you are good, holy, strong, competent, effective, powerful, joyful, wise, hopeful, and all the other qualities that can help you live life as the gift that it is. You received these qualities through the generosity of grace, and grace will reveal them to you whenever you need them. Do not doubt this. Do not resist it. It is true, and this truth will set you free.

Run, don't walk, into the arms of your loving Father who runs down the road to meet you in order to put his rings on your fingers, wrap you in his finest cloak, and show you to the world as his child in whom he is well pleased. Stand up with strength. Be not afraid. And become who you are!

5

Claim Your
Spiritual Rights

Accoording to the American Express Company, "Membership has its privileges." If this can be said about owning a particular brand of credit card, how much more could it be said of being a family member of the Most High God?

Each one of God's children is not only charged with certain responsibilities; we are also granted certain rights. Much of the anxiety we experience in everyday life is a result of not knowing these spiritual rights. Let me explain.

Baptism (spiritual birth) makes us children of God, and because God wants his home to be a loving and orderly home, he gives his children certain chores to do and certain expectations of family life. In brief, we are given what the church calls a threefold mission: to be priests, prophets, and kings.

Priest, Prophet, and King

First, God tells his children that we must be priests. What does that mean? The main job of a priest is to offer sacrifice. So, if we are to be priests, we must be willing to work for the good of the others in our divine family even when that means making some sacrifice of our selves, our effort, or our time. Likewise, we must be willing to help others in their pursuit of becoming the people God created them to be, even when that means risking our comfort or our own preferences. In this way, we become like our First Brother, Jesus Christ, who offered himself in total sacrifice for the good of us all.

Second, God asks his children to be prophets. Many people think that a prophet is someone who tells the future, but that is not what a prophet does (that's a seer). A prophet's job is to pray for wisdom, speak the truth, and stand up for what is just, even in the face of extreme opposition. By making us into prophets, God challenges us to always assert the truth and to stand up for justice. For our purposes, justice means making sure that everyone in our lives—including ourselves—is giving according to his or her ability and receiving according to his or her need. This concept is the key to any healthy, fulfilling Christian relationship because justice, as we are defining it, stands at the heart of respect, without which there can be no intimacy. Similarly, by making us prophets, God also gives us the authority to charitably challenge ourselves and others when they fail to contribute to the level of their ability, and to help those who either can't assert their needs or have a hard time doing so.

Finally, God asks us to remember that we are "kings." As sons and daughters of the Most High God, each one of us is given gifts that we can use in the service of others. Likewise, each one of us is royalty and deserves to be treated with awe and respect. We do not claim this nobility on our own, but by virtue of God's simple generosity. We are royalty because God made it so; but what does it mean to be a king? It means that at all times we must remember our dignity, we must remember the dignity of others in the family, and we must be willing to assert that dignity when others try to treat us in a manner that does not befit our royal status.

And what does all this have to do with anxiety? In chapter 2 we learned that anxiety results primarily from trying to control that which is beyond our ability to control. This is true, but it is also true that much anxiety is caused by not taking charge of that which is within our ability to control. As Reinhold Niebuhr's Serenity Prayer says, "God grant me the serenity to accept what I cannot change, the courage to change what I can, and the wisdom to know the difference." If the secret to serenity is knowing what I can and cannot change, then practicing the threefold mission of priest, prophet, and king is the secret to knowing the difference. Let's look at each one of these missions and how our failure to fulfill them contributes to our experience of anxiety.

Practicing Priesthood

JACK CALLED ME BECAUSE HE WAS EXPERIENCING STRESS AND ANXIETY in his marriage. His wife was threatening to leave him, and he was miserable. "I'm so upset I can't think, I can't sleep, and my work is going down the tubes." As Jack's story unfolded, it became clear that there were long-standing problems in his relationship that he had simply ignored because he didn't want to challenge his comfort zone. His wife had been depressed for a long time, due in part to her history with her family of origin, but due largely to Jack's pattern of neglect and disinterest in his marriage. He often worked long hours, and when he came home he would eat in silence and retire to the television room until he fell asleep. He avoided his wife (except when it came to requests for sex) and even ignored his children, with whom he seemed to have more of an emotionally competitive relationship than anything else.

———

I asked him what he thought the problem was.

"Oh, she's always bitching about something. She always wants me to go with her someplace or 'try new things.' I'm a simple guy; I don't need much. I think a relationship should just happen. It should be natural. Why does she have to make it into such hard work all the time?"

Though Jack was able to avoid it for a long time, the anxiety he was experiencing in the face of his wife's ultimatum was the direct result of his obstinate refusal to fulfill his role as priest toward his wife. True, he worked hard all day, and he made the contributions to their home that he was comfortable making (for example, yard work, car maintenance). Even so, this service was ultimately self-serving because he restricted himself to doing the things that he thought a good husband should do while shutting his eyes to the things his wife needed him to do.

In my talks around the country, I have the opportunity to meet many people who have gained a great deal of hard-won wisdom. Once after a conference, a man cornered me and said, "I really needed to hear what you had to say. It took me twenty-five years to figure out that I wasn't going to get any credit for giving my wife stuff she didn't want."

When I tell that story, many people laugh because they know how true it is. Each one of us tries to play this game with the people we love. We say, "I love you, but I will only love you the way *I* want to love you, so keep your preferences, needs, and wants to yourself."

This is not the priestly love to which we are called. In fact, this "love" is so self-serving that it is really not fit to be called love at all.

To practice the priestly love to which I am called by virtue of my divine sonship means that when someone asks me to do something I am obliged to do it, as long as it does not demean my God-given dignity or offend my moral principles.

How good a priest are you? To find out, take the following quiz. Answer "True" or "False" next to each statement.

HOW GOOD A PRIEST ARE YOU?

Note: If you are not married, substitute the phrase "other people" for "mate" or "children." If you are married, answer the items as they are, because your behavior at home is the clearest indicator of the kind of person you are.

____ Every day, I look for ways to make my mate's life easier or more pleasant.

____ Every day, I look for ways to make my coworkers lives easier or more pleasant.

____ I make a habit of asking my mate and children what they need and responding joyfully to their requests.

____ I do not criticize or make fun of my mate or children for their likes, dislikes, ideas, and interests.

____ I work hard to accommodate my mate's and children's likes, dislikes, ideas, and interests.

____ I encourage my mate and children to do the things that are important to them, even when doing so causes me some inconvenience.

____ I look for opportunities to serve my community (in a way that is respectful of the time I owe to my primary obligations, for example, family, work).

____ The people in my life regularly turn to me for support and encouragement.

____ I do not try to force my own agenda, ideas, or interests on the family. Instead, I solicit theirs and invite them to share mine.

____ In any given situation, I frequently ask myself, "How, specifically, would Jesus want me to respond?" and I work hard to offer that response.

Scoring: Give yourself one point for each statement you marked "True."
Your score: ___ of 10

All of us need to keep striving to fulfill our priestly mission, not only because it benefits the others in our lives, but also because it gives us real power that casts out stress and anxiety. When we willingly and joyfully practice our priesthood, we take control of our relationships.

In Jack's case, he was stressed and miserable because he felt that there was nothing he could do, but this was a prison of his own making. There was nothing he could do because there was nothing he *would* do.

By learning to practice your priesthood, you can escape the prison of powerlessness and celebrate true intimacy in relationships. On the other hand, for those relationships and situations that cause you stress because they undermine your dignity or morality, it is time to practice your prophetic mission.

Fulfilling Your Prophetic Role

MARIANNA WAS A DOORMAT. "No one listens to me. My husband criticizes me constantly; my children are disobedient. I feel like I don't have any control over my own life." It seemed that Marianna was a magnet for difficult people. She had a friend who frequently made unreasonable demands on her (and pouted when Marianna tried to refuse). Her boss took advantage of her generosity, often asking her to stay late to finish his reports while he left early. In response to all this, Marianna was beginning to experience panic attacks in the form of tightness in her chest and shortness of breath. Her doctor had prescribed a popular antianxiety medication and recommended counseling. "I feel lost," she said. "And there is nothing I can do about it."

Marianna's problem consisted largely of her inability to fulfill the prophetic role in her life. Instead of speaking the truth, standing up for just treatment in her home, and insisting that the people in her life contribute according to the level of their ability, she often "stuffed" her feelings, opinions, and ideas for fear of inconveniencing others. She accepted the abuse of others as her just portion and went about cleaning up the messes of others who were more than capable of cleaning up their own messes but simply didn't want to.

Marianna was guided by a false sense of Christian duty, which is to say that she felt it was her job to save the world, or at least the people in her world, from themselves. While we are privileged as priests to offer ourselves in sacrifice for the good of others, that does not mean that we must be doormats. Not even Jesus did all the work for us. He took on the part of our suffering that we could not handle ourselves, but he left us with the part we were capable of bearing. Jesus said to his disciples, "Whoever wishes to come after me must deny himself, take up his cross, and follow me" (Matthew 16:24). That is why we live in what theologians call "the already present but not yet fulfilled Kingdom of God." Thanks to Jesus Christ's saving work, salvation is possible; but thanks to our own incomplete effort, there is still much work to be done.

Most of my work with Marianna consisted of helping her to identify what it meant to be a prophet in her life. Specifically, we mapped out many ways to speak the truth, to stand up for what was just, and to do both in a loving manner. For example, when her husband spoke to her cruelly, Marianna learned to say, "I want to hear what you have to say, but only if you can speak to me respectfully." If her husband persisted in his abusive speech, she would say to him, "When you have calmed down, I will listen, but until then, this conversation is done" and walk away if possible.

Marianna learned to be more effective with her children and

not to succumb to pouting or other forms of emotional extortion regardless of whether it came from her husband, her children, or her demanding friend. She learned to insist charitably that if the people in her life wanted to continue to be in her life, they would treat her with respect, clean up their own messes to the best of their ability, and listen respectfully when she expressed her own thoughts or had to refuse an unreasonable request. Furthermore, she learned how to back up these words with respectful yet assertive actions that did not make the limits she was setting dependent on the other people in her life agreeing with them.

Previously, if her friend Jen made a request of her and Marianna refused, Jen would pout and Marianna would eventually give in. Now, Marianna is able to say confidently, "I am sorry for Jen when she gets upset, and I do whatever I can for her; but my no means no and my yes means yes, and no amount of pouting or pressuring can change that."

To remain within Christian ethics, the prophetic mission must be tied to the priestly mission; otherwise, we appear to be mean and selfish to others. If Marianna simply said that she was no longer going to do anything for her friend, or for that matter, her husband, she would undermine her own credibility and eliminate the possibility that the relationship could become healthier in time. However, since she continued to serve where it was healthy and appropriate but spoke the truth and stood up for what was just, she was able to gain the wisdom to know what she could control and what she shouldn't even try to control.

As a result of this wisdom, Marianna was able to achieve a measure of serenity even before her relationships reflected any change. And in time, all of the people in Marianna's world came to respect—however reluctantly—her prophetic power to speak what was true, to stand up for what was just, and to do both in love.

How good a prophet are you? To find out, take the following quiz. Answer "True" or "False" next to each statement.

HOW GOOD A PROPHET ARE YOU?

Note: If you are not married, answer the items with your most important relationships in mind. If you are married, answer the items with your spouse and children in mind because your behavior at home is the clearest indicator of the kind of person you are.

____ I regularly pray and seek God's wisdom for dealing with stressful relationships and situations.

____ I am confident of my beliefs and ideas, and I am not easily talked out of them when I believe they are true.

____ I know how to assert myself without being disrespectful, mean, or pouty.

____ My yes means yes and my no means no.

____ I know the difference between a reasonable and an unreasonable request.

____ When others do not respect my limits, I know how to back my words up with respectful yet effective action.

____ I am conscientious about helping others as much as possible, but I insist that others do what they are capable of doing to clean up their own messes and solve their own problems.

____ When other people do not fulfill responsibilities they are capable of fulfilling, I do not feel guilty leaving their work undone or letting them experience the consequences of their actions.

____ People respect me as someone who is strong, sensitive, and fair.

____ I am not afraid of conflict.

Scoring: Give yourself one point for each statement you marked "True."
Your score: ____ of 10

Practicing our prophetic mission enables us to proclaim what is true; set respectful limits; refuse requests that are offensive to our personhood, morality, or primary commitments (for example, family or work); insist that others use the gifts they were given to fulfill their responsibilities; and, when connected to our priestly mission, do all of this in a spirit of love and service. This is more than an ideal. It is our inheritance. It is what each of us is to spend our lives figuring out how to do because this is what it means to live a truly Christian life.

As we become more effective people, more actualized Christians, we learn to claim the power that God gives to us and to use this power to overcome the stress and anxiety in our lives. Serenity is possible because (1) our priestly mission empowers us to use our acts of service to change what can be changed, (2) our prophetic role enables us to rely on truth and justice to know what we cannot change ourselves, calls on others to take up their responsibilities, and allows us to set limits with those who do not take up their personal responsibilities, and (3) our kingly mission allows us to rely on the wisdom of the God who gave us our noble office to know the difference. Finally, let's examine the role of king.

What It Means to Be a "King"

BETH ANN DIDN'T KNOW WHAT TO DO. Her husband regularly treated her with contempt and denigrated her with abusive language. He criticized her efforts at housekeeping and called her "weak and whiny" when she would try to keep the peace. He would often tell cruel jokes at her expense in public and private, including bawdy jokes in front of their children. When she complained, he would say, "You're crazy. You need to get a sense of humor."

———

Beth Ann was tearful as she spoke to me. "I tell him how much he is hurting me," she said, "but he doesn't believe me. He just makes fun of me more. I don't think he has ever apologized to me once in our whole marriage. He says his motto is, 'Never apologize, never explain.' I don't want to leave him, but I can't take it anymore."

Sometimes when we try to be prophets, standing up against the injustices we experience and the offenses we encounter, other people dismiss what we have to say. They even mock us and abuse us. This is when it is time to assert our kingly dignity.

The king expects to be treated with the respect of his office. He does not lord his exalted position over others, and a good king knows that he enjoys his position not on his own merits but by the grace of God, whom he attempts to honor in all he does. The king knows that he is deserving of respect because God placed him in a position of respect, but he asserts his dignity in a firm yet charitable manner. The king does not ask permission to be respected; he insists on it. If respect is not forthcoming, he takes action to correct the offense to his person and the offense to the God who gave him his noble office. While not cruel, he is always just and is swift to use his authority to assert the dignity of his office to those who would seek to defame or dethrone him.

We, too, have a noble office. We, too, are infused with dignity and nobility and are raised to the exalted position of "son or daughter of the Most High God." We do not claim this nobility on our own power or merits. After all, we are sinful creatures of whom the psalmist says, "If you, Lord, mark our sins, / Lord, who can stand?" (Psalms 130:3) No, recognizing our unworthiness (as all good kings do), we exalt in the nobility lavished upon us as a free and unmerited gift from our God.

Mystified by the crown God has given us, but confident in it, we are called by God first to treat others in a way that is mindful of their noble bearing. After all, they too are brothers and sisters of the kingdom of God. Second, we are empowered to insist that others treat us with the same dignity and respect with which God treats us. This power extends even to the point of allowing us to take prudent, just, and charitable action when others seek to undermine our God-given dignity.

We often wrestle with this concept. We want to be humble. We think that it is a virtue to act as if we are worthless and that God could never want us to raise our heads. But this is not humility.

To be humble is to recognize how unworthy I am of the gifts I have been given, to be amazed that God would love a creature such as me so much. It is not humble to go so far as deny that I have, in fact, been gifted or am loved. I may not be worthy or lovable on my own merits, but God says that I am worthy and lovable by his merits. This is a great gift in which I can be joyful and confident.

To stand on the promise of my kingship and to insist that I am worthy of respectful treatment is not to be proud. It is to be a child of God. Remember the parable of the talents, in which the man was cast out of the palace because he was afraid to assert the gifts he had been given (Matthew 25:14–30)?

Beth Ann was raised in a home that taught her to accept abusive treatment without question. She carried this lesson into her marriage. Once we worked through the obstacles that stood between her and the ability to claim her divine office, she was able to assert herself with authority to her husband in a way that was clear. She would no longer ask his permission to receive respectful treatment ("Why can't you treat me better?" or "Why do you have to be so cruel?"). She would insist on respectful treatment ("I want to hear what you have to say, but if you cannot speak to me calmly and respectfully, this conversation is over"). When her husband would not listen to her, she learned to take effective, respectful actions that forced him to confront the strength of her resolve head-on.

For example, one time after a particularly offensive outburst, she told him: "I want to be your wife and do all the things a wife does for a husband. But in order to be your wife, you have to treat me with the respect due a wife; otherwise, you make me into little more than a slave and a prostitute, and I will not be that. I am not going to discuss or argue about this with you. When you apologize for your last outburst and begin treating me with the respect I deserve, I will act as your wife. But until then, you will have to fend for yourself."

He was livid. He tried yelling, then pouting, then deflecting. Beth Ann stood firm. For two weeks, she fed the children and herself, but not him. She washed her clothes and the children's clothes, but not his. She picked up the children's things, but not his. If his things were in her way, she put them in a garbage bag and placed them in the garage. She slept in a separate room. And over and over she would remind him, "I want to be your wife and do all the things a wife does for a husband, but, in order for me to be your wife, you must treat me with respect."

After two weeks of this constant repeating and constant resolve, he broke. He apologized sincerely for the first time in their marriage and began going out of his way to be more mindful of her. He agreed to enter counseling with her to resolve their other problems. He acknowledged that he had been abusive in the past and even began attending anger management classes on his own. Today, they are a new couple. She has a newfound strength, and he has true love and respect for her.

Not every situation ends this happily, but that isn't the point. Regardless of the circumstances in which we find ourselves, we are permitted—no, obliged—to assert our God-given dignity even when others do not respect it automatically. We are permitted, by virtue of our God-given kingly office, to take just, prudent, and charitable actions to enforce respectful treatment.

There are those who may object and say, "Jesus was humiliated. He accepted his sufferings passively; why shouldn't I?" But Jesus did not treat all suffering equally. He willingly accepted the suffering necessary to fulfill his ministry, but he actively avoided and even ran away from suffering that was not essential.

Remember when the crowds wanted to stone Jesus, and he "disappeared from their midst"? And even in the Garden of Gethsemane, though Jesus accepted his Father's will, he prayed for his Father to permit him to take a different path if there were any other way for him to accomplish his work. In the end, there was no other way, and Jesus accepted his cross; but he did not do so without seriously reflecting on other, potentially more prudent options.

Sadly, I encounter too many people who accept suffering as their lot because, to be frank, they are too cowardly to take effective action. It is much easier to dress up codependency in pious garb and say, "I'm suffering! See how Christlike I am!" rather than exercise our kingly mission and use God's grace to bring real change to the situation. Jesus exercised his kingship, minding the dignity and worth of his life as he sought the most prudent way to accomplish his mission. We would do well to follow his example.

Once again, our kingly mission contributes to our serenity by making us mindful of our God-given dignity. This mindfulness then helps us distinguish between those times when we must sacrifice for the good of others and those times when we must speak and stand for what is true and just. Likewise, the kingly mission gives us the authority to make these decisions in confidence and to enforce those decisions with just, prudent, and charitable actions.

How good a king are you? To find out, take the following quiz. Answer "True" or "False" next to each statement.

HOW GOOD A KING ARE YOU?

Note: If you are not married, answer the items with your most important relationships in mind. If you are married, answer the items with your spouse and children in mind because your behavior at home is the clearest indicator of the kind of person you are.

___ I am confident in God's love for me.

___ I insist that others treat me with respect.

___ When others do not treat me with respect, I am able to take effective, respectful action to resolve the problem.

___ I carry myself with confidence.

___ I speak with authority on issues I feel strongly about.

___ I do not make threats or promises that I am not prepared to carry out.

___ When problems arise, I am good at figuring out just, prudent, and charitable solutions.

___ I am grateful to God for, and actively use, the gifts and talents he has given me.

___ While open to respectful criticism, I do not tolerate unjust criticism or abuse.

___ I am confident that I know the difference between reasonable and unreasonable requests.

Scoring: Give yourself one point for each statement you marked "True."
Your score: ___ of 10

The Whole Picture

Take a minute to look over the three quizzes you took in this chapter. Write your scores side by side like this (obviously, the higher the score, the more well developed your sense of that particular mission):

Priest _____ Prophet _____ King _____

Your score in the priest category represents your commitment to loving service. Likewise, your score in the prophet category represents your commitment to truth and justice, and your score in the king category represents your commitment to your God-given dignity and confidence in God's love for you.

A high score in the priest category combined with low scores in the prophet and/or king categories suggests that you may contribute to your own anxiety by placing yourself in positions where you are a doormat or where, at least, you take on entirely too much responsibility for other people's problems. Service and sacrifice are good things, and they are the source of much power and change— when used properly. Used imprudently, they are the source of much unnecessary pain and anxiety.

On the other hand, a high score in the prophet and/or king categories combined with a comparatively lower score in the priest category suggests that you may have too great a sense of entitlement. It is good to be confident and to know your rights, but if this comes at the expense of your willingness to serve others generously, you increase anxiety in your life by refusing to do what you can to solve your own problems because "It isn't fair" or "I shouldn't have to do X."

Remember, inner peace is achieved by having the courage to change what you can, the serenity to accept what you cannot, and the wisdom to know the difference. Pursuing growth and balance within and between the three baptismal missions of priest, prophet, and king is your path to power and peace. It is one of the major ways you can make your life and relationships anxiety-resistant.

Finding the golden mean among these three missions is an ongoing balancing act that sometimes can be tricky, but with persistence and a willingness to seek good counsel when necessary, we can achieve success. After all, as sons and daughters of God, to do so is nothing less than our inheritance.

6

Find Where You Left Yourself

CATHY WAS AN UNMARRIED THIRTY-FOUR-YEAR-OLD WOMAN who wanted nothing more in her life than to break free of the anxiety she experienced on an almost daily basis, anxiety that left her too fearful to pursue personally meaningful work or intimate relationships. "As soon as I'm put on the spot—it doesn't matter how—I feel like my face is turning bright red and everybody is staring at me, and I just clam up. I used to just force the anxiety down and try to get through it, but I can't do it anymore."

Raised in a home filled with perfectionism, Cathy was taught that there was a right way and a wrong way to do everything. According to her mother, there was a "best way" to accomplish any task, no matter how menial. And Cathy never seemed to do it well enough to meet her mother's exacting standards.

As a result of the anxiety brought on by her own perfectionist tendencies, Cathy couldn't bring herself to perform in almost any group situation. She would regularly call in sick to the infrequent office meetings she was obliged to attend. She rarely dated ("I start worrying if the guy's going to like me, and I get terrified"). And while she was a talented, self-taught pianist and music gave her great joy, she could not bring herself to play in any public forum, even to the point of being too afraid to take lessons ("I am sure that I would embarrass myself in front of the teacher").

When I asked what she did with her free time, she explained, "Mostly just watch TV. I pray, too, but even that is getting hard. Why does God leave me to suffer like this?"

Leaving Parts Behind

"I'm not all there." It's a common derogatory comment we make about ourselves when we are having emotional problems or suffering from stress that drives us to distraction. We mean it metaphorically, but there is a hidden truth contained within that sentiment. Many times our emotional lives resemble an old jalopy losing parts of itself as it chugs down the road. Somehow, we get from point A to point B, but by journey's end we are not entirely intact.

The result, of course, is that we experience a sense of anxiety that comes from not having enough of our internal resources available to meet the external challenges we face. As time goes by and we encounter more and more crises, more and more pieces of ourself fall off and are left lying on the side of the road. The more this happens, the more anxious we become, because less and less of ourself remains in the present moment to manage the problems we encounter today.

Why does this happen?

Imagine that you and I have an argument, and you say something that just stops me in my tracks. I don't know what to say in response. Chances are, we will part company and we will both get on with our lives. But a week later, as I am driving to work, a thought will hit me. "That's what I should have said!" I have thought of a response to your comment, and though I may be kicking myself for not having said it at the time, I can finally have closure to our argument.

Why did I have that delayed reaction to our discussion? Because even though most of my mind moved on after our frustrating conversation, I left a small part of my unconscious self "back there" in that discussion with you. Something you said made an impression; you made a comment that I didn't know how to assimilate, or you challenged me with a question I couldn't answer. But humans hate loose ends. If someone claps out, "Shave and a hair cut . . ." and then stops, odds are that there will not be a single person in the room who does not, at least internally, complete the phrase: "—two bits!" We just can't let it go. In the same way, unanswered questions drive us to distraction.

Consider the example of our argument again. After you made that comment, the conscious part of me moved on through time and became a week older, so to speak. But at least one part of my unconscious mind remained stuck in that past moment. It is as if that one offended part of my mind said to the rest of me: "Oh, that's all right, you go ahead; I'll catch up with you later. I have some work to finish up." It then sat down on the side of the road and kept saying to itself, "Could I have said *this*? Should I have said *that*?"

My conscious mind might be completely unaware that this is going on, save for a mild, unidentifiable sense of unease that comes from the fact that part of me has gone missing. But that one little part of my mind will remain there, a week in the past, turning that question over and over until, "Eureka! I've got the answer!" It then runs at the speed of thought to catch up with my conscious self and passes on its epiphany to the rest of my mind— whereupon I hit myself in the head for not thinking of such a great zinger sooner. Nevertheless, it's good news for me. My mind is reintegrated and internal peace is restored as all the parts of my mind have caught up with each other.

Unfinished Business

If this can occur with something as common as a simple disagreement, imagine how much of ourselves we can leave behind when something truly serious happens: when, as a five-year-old, I can't figure out why Mommy keeps telling me that I am a bad boy even though I am trying my best to please her; when I can't understand why, as an elementary school child, I never seem to get anything right as far as my dad is concerned; when I don't understand why my parents had to get a divorce and how I can get them back together again; when I can't understand why I keep getting beaten by my drunken father or why my peers never accept me at school no matter how hard I try. Or a million other possibly traumatic or personally hurtful events.

When we go through difficult times such as these, we leave parts of ourselves behind to struggle with unanswered questions: "Why did this happen to me?" "What should I have said?" "What could I have done differently?" "How can I get them to love me?" "How can I make the hurt stop?" "When will I get to feel like I can do something right?" "Who will tell me when I am finally good enough?"

These questions sap our energy and prevent us from being able to attend to our present-day problems and concerns with all our resources intact. Because so much of ourselves is left behind to work on what psychotherapist Fritz Perls called "unfinished business," we end up feeling the same anxiety about daily life as we would feel if someone commanded us to run a marathon with one leg tied behind our back.

Do you often feel as though you are running on a treadmill and can't get off? Do you feel driven to prove yourself to someone or something, but you don't know to whom or what? Do you feel like a fraud in your everyday life, as if someone is going to discover that you are really only six years old and tell you that you shouldn't be doing whatever it is you are doing? Are you consumed by fears that strike you as stupid and silly when you actually think about them, but are all consuming when you are experiencing them? Do you have a difficult time making decisions because you are never sure what the "right" answer is? Do you frequently feel as if you are on the outside of life looking in and are tormented with the anxiety that comes from life passing you by faster than you can catch it?

If you answered yes to any of these questions, chances are that you have left a part of yourself behind. This part has become, as Freud put it, fixated with answering particular, ontological questions that will not let you move forward in life until they are adequately addressed.

Erin's Story

ERIN WAS TERRIFIED TO BE ALONE AT NIGHT, a problem that was made worse since her husband was for the first time in their married lives pulling the night shift at the power plant where he was a safety systems coordinator. A very functional thirty-two-year-old woman by day,

Erin became unglued every night when her husband left for work. She was so consumed with the fear of being alone that she would practically barricade herself in her room, refusing to come out, even to go to the bathroom—especially remarkable since she was six months pregnant at the time.

———————

"I know it's crazy," she said, acknowledging that most grown women did not share her experience, "but I can't control the fear. It just takes me over, almost as if I am a completely different person. The adult, rational part of me goes on vacation, and these crazy feelings take me over and I can't do anything about it except give in to them."

Erin experienced a moderate degree of relief from the cognitive techniques described in chapter 2, but the fear still impaired her nighttime comfort. We decided to go deeper and investigate the possibility that she had left a part of herself somewhere along the way and that this part was calling out to be reunited with her adult self. I asked her to reflect on the following question and give the first answer that came into her head without judging or analyzing the answer: "Assuming that the part of you that is afraid is not your adult, thirty-two-year-old self, how old is the part of you that experiences the nighttime fear?"

After a brief moment of confusion, and my encouragement that the answer didn't have to make sense, she said, "Eight years old springs to mind; I don't know why."

I asked Erin to reflect on that time in her life. Where did she live? What was her home like then? How was her relationship with her parents, her peers? Were there any significant events that occurred at that time that might be the source of some stress for an eight-year-old girl?

Erin began describing her middle childhood. She lived in a depressed section of town. Her mother, a poor, single mom, worked as a waitress at a local truck stop. Shortly after Erin's eighth birthday, her mother deemed her old enough to baby-sit her five-year-old brother and three-year-old sister while she went out on dates, since "the little kids would be sleeping, and I was supposed to be in bed by nine o'clock anyway."

"I remember being terrified of every noise in the house," Erin said. "I would make my brother and sister get in bed with me. I read them a story and waited until I was sure they were asleep. Then I would block the door with a chair and sit up in bed all night, sometimes with the covers pulled up tight around my head and only my eyes sticking out. I would lie awake waiting until I heard my mom come home. I would look out the window to make sure it was her car, and then I would tiptoe to the door and put the chair back and pretend to be asleep when she checked in. I was afraid that if she ever found the chair there she would whip me for not being a big girl."

This ritual continued several nights a week until Erin's tenth birthday, when her mother remarried and began staying home at night. I suggested to Erin that she had left a part of her mind back there in her childhood home, lying awake with her brother and sister beside her and the chair against the door. That part of her mind had stayed behind to struggle over and over with questions like: "What can I do to make sure no one comes and gets me?" "When is Mommy coming home?" "What if my brother or sister gets sick and I can't help them?" "What if somebody breaks into the house and kills me?" "What if space aliens come and get me and cut me up?" (This was one of her biggest fears as a child, introduced by an episode of a popular television series that she had accidentally seen.)

I suggested that every night, when Erin's husband left, that eight-year-old child became terrified again. Terrified of being alone, of being vulnerable. I suggested that this little girl needed to know that she was safe, that she had survived and never had to be afraid again.

Erin later confided, "I thought you were crazy when you first told me that. But the more I thought about it, the more it seemed like the only possible explanation. I know that the average thirty-two-year-old woman doesn't feel like I do, and that thirty-two-year-old people know better than to be afraid of the dark, especially in the comfort of their own homes. It was obvious that it was a childish, childhood fear, but I didn't want to admit it—especially the space-alien thing—because I felt foolish hanging onto that all this time."

Having decided that we had achieved at least a workable hypothesis, I asked her if she would be willing to do an experiment. At night, when she was alone and afraid, I asked her to imagine that she really was eight and that her mommy was out on a date. She was all alone in the house with her siblings in bed with her, and they were depending on her for protection. I asked her to write a note, in child's handwriting, describing her fears to her adult self.

Once she had completed the note, I asked her to take a breath to clear her head. Then I asked her to reread the note as her adult thirty-two-year-old self. Finally, I had her write back to the child, responding to the fears as if her own daughter had expressed them. Here is what Erin wrote.

> Dear Grown-up Erin,
>
>   I feel scared. I'm afraid somebody's going to get me and my mommy's going to be dead or something. I'm all alone and scared and it isn't fair that I have to take care of my brother and sister by myself. I'm all alone and I want to cry and cry. Help me.
>
>   Little Erin

Dear Little Erin,

I know how afraid you are. After all, a long time ago, I used to be you. But I want you to know that you make it through that time in your life. No one comes to get you. No one wants to hurt you. And even though it isn't fair that your mom is asking you to do this very grown-up job, you took good care of James and Brenda, and I am proud of how brave you are.

I want you to know that you are not eight anymore. I grew up and you are inside of me, so you are a grown-up, too, even if sometimes you don't feel like one. And where I am, there is nothing to be afraid of anymore. I know that God loves me and is taking care of us, and I have a husband who loves me, and I am having a little baby girl. Life is very good here in this time. I am a grown woman now, and I can take care of myself and I can take care of you.

I love you very much and I am proud of you. Come and stay with me and let me take care of you. At night, remember that I am here, and you are safe with me. God loves you, and so do I. You are a good girl, and Jesus doesn't want you to be afraid anymore. Trust him. Trust me. And sleep tight, little one.

Love,

Grown-up Erin

For the next part of the exercise, I had Erin imagine her eight-year-old self sitting across from her. I asked the adult Erin in front of me to talk to the child Erin and explain the things that she wrote in the letter and ask her child self if she had any other questions. One by one, the questions came out, and "adult Erin" patiently answered them from the perspective of an adult who, twenty-four years earlier, had gone through experiences similar to this child's.

Then I asked Erin to imagine taking this child self in her arms and holding her close. Adult Erin promised this child self that she would take care of her, and told the child that any time she felt afraid, instead of taking over the adult Erin, she was to simply whisper in the adult Erin's ear and ask for some reassurance. In these times, it would be the adult Erin's job to remember that it was not she who was feeling fearful but the child self who needed the adult to comfort her. After all, in her worst moments alone in her room, there was nothing that would intimidate the adult Erin, only the child self who should never have been left alone in the first place.

Finally, the adult Erin was to imagine holding the child self close and comforting her in her arms. As the warmth increased between the two of them, Erin was to bring the child self back inside of her, taking up a warm, safe place close to her heart, where she could be completely surrounded by the love and protection the adult Erin could offer her.

Following this exercise, I instructed Erin that if her child self felt anxious in the future, she should either repeat the visualization or do another exchange of letters between the two. Here is what Erin had to say about her experience:

"I wasn't sure what to make of the exercise when you took me through it at first, but that night I wasn't nearly as fearful as I had been. Frankly, I was surprised by how peaceful I felt."

When the nervousness began creeping back, Erin would remind herself that it was her child self, not her adult self, who was nervous, and that here, in the present, there was nothing to fear. Likewise, if her child self needed reassurance, she was more than capable of providing it. She added, "My anxiety has decreased to the point where I can do what I need to do at night whether my husband is there or not."

Tips for Picking Up the Pieces

It is often difficult for a person to complete this technique fully without the assistance of a therapist trained in this method, but you can at least start the process of reintegrating the parts of yourself you have lost along the way.

1. **Recognize when you are battling the child self.**
   Our adult selves become anxious about things that are happening in the present. While these fears and anxieties may not always be rational, they are at least understandable. By contrast, our child selves often feel anxious, driven, or fearful about things that either do not make sense to us, are beyond our immediate conscious awareness, or are resistant to our conscious attempts to correct them.

   For example, you may exhibit a certain problem behavior or emotional state that causes you to become frustrated with yourself. Having gotten through that behavior or emotional state, you promise yourself sincerely, "I am never going to allow myself to behave that way again." But sure enough, a week later, it is as if your adult, rational self goes on vacation and the idiot comes out in you, making you do the very same thing all over again.

   You may be aware of it; you may even be able to watch yourself doing it, all the while commenting, "This is stupid, I should stop." But at the same time you may feel completely powerless to control yourself. Once that moment passes, you may experience a letdown; for example, you may be overcome by feelings of depression or guilt, at which point you say, "I can't believe I went there again! What is wrong with me?" Chances are that what is "wrong" with you is that you are dealing not with a problem of your adult self relating to your present world, but with a problem of your child self struggling through a past crisis.

2. **Ask yourself, "How old does this part of me feel?"**
   You may have a difficult time accepting this notion just yet. That's all right. Just play along for the time being. No harm can come to you even if you think this is silly. Having identified that your anxiety or stress may not be coming from your adult self, we need to know at what point in your personal history your child self is fixated.

   Imagine that you could ask the part of you that is anxious or stressed how old it is. Accept whatever age pops into your head; it doesn't have to make sense right now.

3. **If you identified an age, ask yourself, "What was going on at this time in my life?"**
   Having made a guess at a possible age, ask yourself, "What major stressors was I encountering?" "What were my relationships with my peers, parents, or other family members like?" and other questions that could reveal the source of the present behavior or emotional reaction.

4. **Write a letter that expresses the major questions or fears that were present at this time from this child self to your present self.**
   Allow yourself to express the frustration and questions of this past time in your life as fully as possible. What does your child self need to know in order to experience some sense of relief or resolution about that time? Make sure that this letter expresses those concerns to the adult self.

5. **Respond as your adult, rational self to the child self.**
   Getting back in touch with the adult you of the present,
   reread the letter from the child self. Remember when, as a
   child, you used to feel this way. Write a letter to the child
   self. Share the lessons you have learned along the way
   that would be helpful. Imagine asking yourself, "What do
   I wish some caring, attentive adult had told me when I
   was that age?" Allow your adult self to leave that difficult
   time behind.

6. **Continue the dialogue.**
   It is rarely enough to do this exercise once. Often it begins
   an ongoing dialogue between your adult and child selves
   that, while ultimately ending in integration, may take some
   time. If the questions or concerns your child self is
   expressing are fairly mild, you may be able to resolve the
   issues holding you back fairly quickly. If, on the other hand,
   your child self is responding to a pattern of abuse, neglect,
   criticism, rejection, or other painful emotional wounding
   that lasted over a period of years, this process will take
   longer. Depending on the severity and duration of the
   childhood experiences that caused the wound, you may
   wish to seek professional guidance to help your child self
   find the peace and integration that is presently missing.

Gary's Story

GARY IS A DRIVEN CAREER MAN. A leader of his sales team for a major manu-
facturing firm, he enjoys the benefits of his success. The one draw-
back? He can't ever relax. "People talk about burning the candle at

both ends. Somewhere along the line, I just threw the whole damn candle into the fire. I love my work and I'm good at it, but I can't let it go. Every time I think about cutting back, it's like I hear my old man shouting in my head that I won't amount to anything. It drives me. I know it's crazy, but sometimes I feel like my whole life is devoted to proving him wrong."

———————

Gary regularly spent at least seventy hours a week at the office and another twenty to thirty hours a week working at home. In addition to the obvious marital and family tension his behavior caused, he was frustrated with his company, which was not rewarding the level of effort he was giving to the job. Gary felt that his employers were taking advantage of him. They knew that he was willing to put in as much time as it took to get the job done, so they were reluctant to hire people who could make his job easier. Likewise, Gary had made several arrangements with immediate supervisors that upon the completion of a particular project, he would be promoted to a more lucrative and less stressful position. Unfortunately, an odd series of events found these managers being moved to different departments or leaving the company before the projects were completed, and the new managers were reluctant to make good on the verbal agreements Gary had made with their predecessors.

Gary told me, "I feel like a gerbil on a wheel. But I can't stop because the whole thing could come crashing down, and I owe it to myself and my employer to make this work."

Even so, there was a part of Gary that knew his behavior was irrational. "I went to a retreat, and the leader asked us what the most important things in our lives were. I said 'God and my family,' but I knew that was a lie. I *want* God and my family to be my priority, but the truth is that I don't have time for them. I know that isn't right, but I don't know how to stop."

Gary frequently beat himself up for his "messed-up priorities," but his conscious attempts to correct his behavior always failed. He would make promises to change, pencil in family time on his schedule, make commitments to his wife and children, and do all this with sincerity of heart. But then a last-minute meeting would appear, or a client would call just as he was heading out the door. Or he would be "almost done" with a project and "just need another thirty minutes to finish up"; three hours later he would head home with a mixture of guilt and self-hatred that would inevitably be expressed as irritation with his family.

I suggested to Gary that while he was struggling with a serious problem, this might not be an issue with his adult self. I explained the process described in this chapter and asked him how old the part of him was that might be responsible for his driven-ness.

At first he resisted the idea. "I don't see how what happened to me as a kid could have anything to do with my work. I wasn't working in an office when I was a kid."

I explained to Gary that he may have learned lessons that affected his present relationships and his drive for approval, the manner in which he manages his time, and his almost desperate need to prove himself. I told him that this line of inquiry might not bear any fruit, but that it was my job to rule out all the possible factors contributing to his stress. I repeated my request that he ask the part of himself that would not let him relax how old it was.

"I don't know. Sixteen comes to mind."

Gary and I talked about this time in his life, and though there were certain events that could have been clinically significant, it became clear to me that his driven-ness had already been well in place by age sixteen. I suggested he ask this sixteen-year-old part of himself whether this was the first time in his life that he felt so driven, or if the problem started even earlier.

A confused look spread across Gary's face. He said, "Six comes to mind, but I don't know why."

I told Gary to stay with that age for a minute, to just let his mind wander and allow his child self to show him why this age was so significant. All at once, he started to tear up. His brother, he told me, was ten years older and the star of the family. "Everything always seemed to come easy to him. He was a great student. Real popular, and though my dad would never admit it to my face, I always knew he was my dad's favorite."

As Gary talked, a powerfully painful experience came back to him. At six, his teachers noticed that he was having some learning problems. They recommended a battery of psychological and educational tests to diagnose the nature of his mild learning disability. Gary recalled that when he brought the note home from his teachers, his father became furious—not with him, necessarily, but inexplicably angry nevertheless. Gary's mother tried to intervene, and Gary's father told him to go up to his room and wait.

"I thought maybe I had done something wrong. I wanted to hear what they were saying, so I pretended to stomp up the stairs and close my door hard, but really I stayed at the landing at the top of the steps. I heard my dad yelling at my mom."

Gary stopped for a moment to try to compose himself. "I heard my dad say, 'I never wanted another one. You kept harping on me for years, and now I've got to put up with some retard for the rest of my life!'"

Gary didn't stick around to hear any more as he quietly slipped into his room and closed the door. He never mentioned what he heard to his parents, and they never discussed the matter with him. He had his testing, which revealed a mild auditory processing problem. But by then Gary had made up his mind that he wasn't going to give his parents an excuse to reject him.

"I killed myself studying from first grade on. I always asked for extra-credit work. I asked the teacher for extra help. I tried to help out at school so the teacher would like me. I read as much as I could, and even though I was never a great student, I worked my butt off to be the best I could. I don't know if my dad would even remember saying that. He always said stuff when he was angry. But I remember crying myself to sleep the night I found out that not only was I never wanted, but I was stupid, too."

Later, Gary wrote a letter from his six-year-old child self to his adult self expressing his grief over this time in his life.

> Dear Grown-up Gary,
>
> I feel so sad. Dad thinks I'm dumb and he said they didn't want me. Why? What did I do to make them so mad at me? Why does my dad have to say such mean things all the time? I hate him. I have to show him I'm not dumb. I don't ever want anybody to think I'm stupid.
>
> I'm tired though. I've been trying so hard for a long time to make them happy. And they're still not. Nothing I do is good enough for them. When will they love me the way I want them to? I'm so sad.
>
> Little Gary

In the course of writing this letter, Gary had an important insight. It dawned on him that when it came to his present-day work behavior, he identified his company with his father. It was as if he saw his dad's head on his employer's body. He settled for the same treatment from his employer as he had accepted from his father. Likewise, he realized that he was killing himself to win the approval of a boss who would never give it, just as little Gary drove himself to perform in order to win his withholding father's approval. All at once, it occurred to him that neither of these painful sources of pressure was his relationship or his responsibility.

We discussed these insights in Gary's next session, and I helped him craft his adult self's response to the child.

Dear Little Gary,

I know how sad you are. I was once in the same situation that you are in. I want you to know that I grew up, and everything is going to be OK for you, too, because I am going to help you learn the things I have discovered since I was your age.

I know that you think it is your fault that your dad is angry, but it's not. I know you think that it's your fault that your mom and dad don't love you the way that you wish they did, but it's not. See, just like someone can have a broken leg or a broken arm, some people can have the part of them that loves broken or sprained. If that happens to a person, that person tries to love as much as they know how, but it won't seem like enough to the people around them, and those people will feel sad, just like you do.

That's the way Dad was, and Mom, too. They tried their best, but somebody else broke that part of them that could love you as well as you needed to be loved. That wasn't their fault, and it wasn't yours either. You asked me why Dad said such mean things. Well, remember when you broke your arm, and you said all those bad words to your coach? You liked your coach. You didn't want to be mean. But you hurt so badly that you couldn't stop yourself from saying those things, even though you didn't want to.

That's the way your dad felt most of the time. The person who said those things wasn't really your dad. The person who said those things was the hurt, scared little kid inside of him, just like you are the hurt, scared kid inside of me.

I want the hurt to stop. I want you to know that I love you. You have proven yourself over and over again. But even if you never did,

I would still love you, because you are God's child, and he loves you so much. You don't have to prove anything to him or me. I want to be the grown-up you look to for approval, reassurance, and love— not my employer, not my parents, not anybody else, because nobody understands you as well as I do, except God, and I will introduce you to him, too. I promise to be here to reassure you whenever you start feeling crazy inside. From now on, I am going to be here to make you take a break when you get too worked up, because I know it's too hard for you to stop on your own. I love you, and I want to work together with you to help you be free to play and enjoy life like the kid you are.

    Grown-up Gary

This was only the beginning of Gary's powerful and transformative dialogue with his child self. Over the course of several weeks, using this and other techniques to strengthen his bond with this previously lost part of himself, it became easier for him to set limits with his work.

One time he reported that as he was leaving the office, the phone rang. His caller ID showed that it was an important client, but he had already spoken with the client earlier that day and didn't have anything new to report. So he let the phone ring as he walked out of the office. He had never done this before, but he wanted to be home on time for a change.

When I asked him how he managed it, Gary told me that he imagined his child self wanting to pick up the phone just in case he would hear Daddy's approving voice. He imagined himself reminding the child that Dad wasn't calling; it was just a client. "I told him [Gary's child self] that he needed to come home with me so that he could play with my kids." Gary smiled conspiratorially. "He liked that idea."

Eventually Gary found the courage to leave the company and start his own consulting business at home, something he had always wanted to do but was too afraid to try before. He left behind the desperate need for approval that had kept him stuck in his previous workplace.

Together Again

As you've seen throughout the chapter, stress often comes from having left pieces of ourselves on the side of life's highway. The more integrated we are or the more we work to become integrated, the more of ourselves we have available in the present moment to deal effectively, rationally, and proactively with the challenges we face each day.

By using the techniques presented in this chapter, you can begin to reintegrate the pieces of yourself you have left behind. Sometimes, however, you may need a therapist trained in this method to support you in your journey.

7

Practice Joy

Some people have said that when anxiety comes in the door, joy flies out the window. Curiously, though, I have found that people who make a habit of practicing joy often experience less anxiety, or at least less-intense levels of anxiety, than their more serious, nose-to-the-grindstone counterparts.

I believe the reason for this is that joy is one of the most primal ways God reveals himself to us. When we allow ourselves to practice joy, we allow ourselves to become the kind of little children God calls us to be—grateful for all the gifts he gives, trusting in his providence and generosity, and even fearless, because we know our *Abba* daddy is there to catch us when we fall.

Many Christians are suspicious of joy. They feel that joy will somehow interfere with all that penance they should be doing, so they treat joy as that guilty pleasure among the spiritual gifts— something they can participate in now and then just as long as they don't enjoy it too much or tell anyone else about it!

But joy has a long history in the Judeo-Christian tradition. An old Jewish proverb says "God will hold us responsible for all the permitted pleasures we fail to enjoy." When Christmas happened to fall on a Friday, a traditional fast day, St. Francis was asked by his brothers whether they should fast or feast. The beloved saint is said to have replied, "On such a day as this, it is my desire that even the walls should be smeared with meat so that they may feast."

As Christians, we need to take joy out of mothballs and celebrate it as our birthright. Jesus "came so that [we] might have life and have it more abundantly" (John 10:10). You would be hard-pressed to deny that joy is an integral part of living abundantly. It also happens to play a central role in God's plan for protecting us from all anxiety.

Joy vs. Happiness

To begin with, we need to distinguish between joy and mere happiness. Happiness is a transient condition that comes and goes as it pleases. And while pleasant, happiness is not always virtuous. For example, my happiness usually depends on my comfort, but comfort is often the archenemy of love. I have met many a couple in which one spouse is happy and the other is not, because the happy spouse is only willing to love the other to the degree that he is comfortable doing so. He maintains his own happiness by, in effect, emotionally starving his mate to death, all the while blaming her for her misery. "I'm happy and you're not. Obviously you have the problem, not me."

Joy, by contrast, being a gift of the Holy Spirit, is always a virtue, and though it is often accompanied by happiness, it is much bigger. Joy is the virtue that allows us to experience an all-encompassing sense of wonder and awe at God's creation and the gifts he has given us. Joy allows us to be playful in a way that is also respectful of our responsibilities. While happiness tells us to seek it by abandoning our work, joy tells us to pursue the deeper satisfaction of a job well done.

Joy is that gift that allows us to have a healthy sense of humor. While happiness often goes for the cheap or hurtful laugh, joy gives birth to a kind of humor that can be wry at times, but always makes our burden lighter.

When I make happiness my ultimate goal, I limit myself to only those activities and experiences that I find comfortable, leading to a very small life indeed. Likewise, pursuing mere happiness can often lead to loneliness, because other people may ask me to do things that make me uncomfortable. If I refuse them, eventually they will tire of my company and leave me, and I will be alone with my small but comfortable life.

Joy, on the other hand, challenges us to live a more abundant life. It asks us to seek more, to try new things, to open ourselves to new experiences, and to expose ourselves to all of God's creation in all of its messy glory. Joy also draws us into deeper, more intimate relationships with others as it calls us out of ourselves and makes us more active players in our relationships, our community, and our world.

The Joy Connection

Ironically, the pursuit of joy can often involve some degree of discomfort. Opening ourselves up to joy means challenging our limits, expanding our comfort zones, "living large," and taking risks, all so that God might give us a more abundant life in him. Ultimately, though, joy extracts a small, short-term fee for an incredibly long-term gain, a gain that includes love, intimacy, peace, fulfillment, and a true Christian happiness to boot.

When joy is coursing through our veins, we are connected to God, to his providence, and to the wonders of his creation. It's like a shot that the Divine Physician administers in the hope of inoculating us against stress. When we are connected to joy, we can see how, as St. Paul says, "If God is for us, who can be against us?" (Romans 8:31).

Of course, the time to go and get our inoculation is not when we are already in the throes of the disease. In order for joy to work as an insulator against stress, we must practice it every day and build our lives around it. To quote St. Paul again: "Rejoice always. Pray without ceasing. In all circumstances give thanks" (1 Thessalonians 5:16–18).

Before going further, take a moment to assess the level of joy in your life with this quiz. Answer "True" or "False" next to each statement.

HOW JOYFUL ARE YOU?

___ I regularly try new things.

___ I look for ways to be playful with the people in my life.

___ My family and friends enjoy my sense of humor.

___ Throughout the day, I thank God for the little blessings that I encounter.

___ I enjoy learning about things I have never tried before.

___ I make a "happy fuss" (as opposed to a "stressed-out fuss") about birthdays, anniversaries, holidays, and other special occasions.

___ I regularly make appropriately humorous comments that lighten the mood and brighten the people around me.

___ I regularly find small ways to show the people in my life that they are special to me.

___ I am a physically affectionate person.

___ Every day I take time to meditate on and thank God for the blessings in my life.

Your score: ____ of 10

Scoring:
0–3 Bah, humbug! You are in desperate need of a joy infusion.
4–5 Although there is some joy in your life, you probably don't spend a great deal of time cultivating it. Pay attention to the suggestions in this chapter in order to insulate yourself more effectively against stress and worry.
6–7 You make a conscientious effort to practice joy in your life. Build on your strengths with the suggestions in this chapter.
8+ You are the joy master! (Can I be your friend?)

Now, let's take a look at exactly how joy defends us from stress and also how we can cultivate a greater sense of this precious gift of the Spirit.

Cultivating Joy

Think of joy as a tank. I feel healthiest and most connected to God when my tank is full, and I fill the tank by practicing joy, using some of the strategies we are about to discuss. By the same token, stress and anxiety siphon off the joy in my tank. The relationship between the two is like the relationship between a jug of ice water and a scorching, hot day. I can still get thirsty, but as long as I don't let the jug run dry, I will never be too thirsty. In a similar fashion, the key to keeping the heat of stress off my back is to keep the cool waters of joy close at hand.

There are many ways to keep the joy tank full. Let's take a close look at six of them.

1. **Seek out new experiences.**
Studies consistently show that burnout is one of the primary causes of work and life stress. Burnout is the

mind-numbing sense of "been there, done that" that saps
our joy and makes the tasks of our daily life a drudgery.
New challenges, new opportunities, and new experiences
are essential for joyful living. Most of us can't make radical
changes in our career or station in life, but we can seek out
new experiences, we can learn more creative ways to do
what we are already doing, and we can challenge ourselves
to do something that is entirely unlike ourselves.

Recently, a number of women in a local Catholic
homeschooling group (my wife included) enrolled in, of all
things, a belly-dancing class. No doubt when you imagine
the sort of people who would populate a belly-dancing
class, Catholic homeschoolers don't immediately leap to
mind. But that was exactly the point. It was different, out
of the ordinary, fun, challenging, and a little bit silly. There
was little danger of any of these women going professional,
but that, again, was the point.

Too many of us limit ourselves to what we are
comfortable doing. We never expand our boundaries and
discover all the abilities God has buried within us. We try
to practice joy by doing more of the things we are used to
doing. We take music lessons, we play sports, we read
good books. Fine. But I am suggesting that while these
things are good, they are not enough. To be a master at
the art of joy is to look for entirely new flavors to try, to
do the unusual thing, to say, "Oh, I don't think I am the
sort of person who would enjoy *that*" and then do it
anyway. It is exactly this willingness to step outside of the
box in which you live that opens you to joy, because it
opens you up to the abundant variety of blessings that
God has built into life.

Human beings need challenges. God created us to grow. Psychologists call this drive to become more than we are our "actualizing tendency" and say that it is hard-wired into each of us. Those individuals who embrace this actualizing tendency are healthy, vibrant, joyful people. Those individuals who avoid it, choosing mere comfort and "happiness" instead, in the end find little of either as their lives shrink and they become suffocated by their own tiny existence.

I encourage you to constantly look for ways to challenge your competencies, expand your horizons, and do those things that really "aren't you." Assuming that an activity isn't offensive to your moral sense or your personal dignity, why hold yourself back?

The next time your mate asks you to do something out of the ordinary, something that causes you to leave your comfort zone, the next time you are struck by a whim or something tickles your fancy, follow it through. Risk the silly, uncomfortable feeling that comes with leaving behind your teeny, tiny known world. Live life more abundantly. Fill up your joy tank and reap the reward of a more joyful, stress-resistant life.

2. Nurture your playfulness.

By "playfulness" I don't mean "escapism," which is an irresponsible play that takes us away from being the people we are, doing the work we are called to do, and reaching out to the people in our lives. Individuals who are dedicated to pursuing comfort and mere happiness are extremely prone to escapism. They often take the path of least resistance through life, which leads to choices they may live to regret and precious little resolve to correct those choices in a healthy, proactive way.

Playfulness, unlike escapism, is a "true" kind of play, because it leads us to greater appreciation and participation in the life we have and draws us into deeper relationships with the people who share our lives. The playful person looks for opportunities to celebrate life throughout the day.

Jennifer is such a person. Each day, she puts a little note in her children's lunches. She looks for holidays to celebrate, including Catholic holy days, on which she usually makes a special meal and does something small to commemorate the occasion with her husband and children. Almost every day, Jennifer and her husband, Peter, take time to be with their children through activities that build a sense of togetherness and joy—playing a game, doing a craft project, reading aloud to each other. The family uses Sundays as their family day, which revolves around some kind of activity like a picnic, cooking a meal together, a movie (even if it's just a video and popcorn in the family room), a day trip to a local attraction, or something else that makes the day special for everyone. Peter often takes the lead in planning periodic dates, making baby-sitting arrangements as well as suggesting possible activities. As Jennifer put it, "Sharing times like these draws us closer together and helps us resist all the outside pressure that pulls us apart."

Whether we are in a family or not, true playfulness draws us into deeper community with the people who share our lives. Sometimes it takes real work. While the kind of playfulness I am describing does not require us to be cheerful and bouncy at all times (God forbid!), it does require us to find ways to connect with others, to reach out and make their lives more enjoyable. Life is serious business most of the time, but play is an important part of living an abundant, joyful life.

Before we go on to the next point, take a moment to think of ten simple things that bring you closer to the people in your life. Ask yourself which activities you have enjoyed with someone, what kind of humor the people in your life appreciate, and what little celebrations you have participated in or planned in the past that you could reenact starting today. Let these be your jumping off point for bringing more playfulness into your life, and start celebrating the peace and joy (and decreased stress) that will follow.

3. Foster a healthy sense of humor.

Joy also manifests itself in a healthy sense of humor about ourselves, our relationships, and life in general. Not that life is one big sitcom for people who practice joy, but joyful people work to find the fun where they can.

Maria especially loves her husband's ability to make her laugh when she's stressed. "Sometimes when I am totally fried, he'll put his arms around me and start singing that Monty Python song 'Always Look on the Bright Side of Life' in a hackneyed Russian accent. It's the stupidest thing in the world, but I laugh every time."

A good sense of humor is a sign of mental health. The American Psychiatric Association's *Diagnostic and*

Statistical Manual of Mental Disorders (a book that is every bit as fun as it sounds) describes the defensive functioning scale, which rates all the various "defense mechanisms" (ways that people mentally guard themselves from being overwhelmed by stress) from least to most healthy. In the healthiest category, along with other high-level mechanisms such as proactivity, self-awareness, altruism, and help-seeking, is sense of humor.

Humor gives perspective and bonds people together. It decreases our emotional temperature, so that we can find solutions that are less obvious to a person under stress. When you laugh with another person, you are reminded that even in stress you are teammates. And in a marriage, even the simplest, well-timed joke can stop a couple from reenacting their favorite scenes from *The Exorcist* when what they really need to be doing is having a healthy problem-solving session.

A sense of humor is one of those things that people think you either have or you don't, but this isn't true. For example, comedian Drew Carey, in an interview on National Public Radio's *Fresh Air,* said that he didn't know how to write a joke until he read a self-help book that described how to be funny. At first I thought he was kidding, but he assured the interviewer several times that he was quite serious.

The best kind of humor uplifts you and the people around you. It is perfectly fine to make fun of your situation or even of yourself at times. It is rarely, if ever, appropriate to make derogatory comments about another person just for a cheap laugh. Granted, some element of teasing is part and parcel of any relationship, but sometimes even the most innocent joke at someone's expense can seriously damage a relationship. Some people bristle when their listeners are offended by a failed attempt at humor. We need to remember that one of the most important rules of healthy humor is that a joke is only funny if both the person telling the joke and the person hearing the joke agree that it is funny.

For some people, a positive and uplifting sense of humor is a natural gift. And then there are others, like me, who seem to have inherited a gene for "curmudgeon-liness" and have to work a little harder. Either way, filling your life with laughter can be as simple as breaking into some act of spontaneous silliness (like grabbing your mate and dancing your version of the Hustle just to be a pest), or making frequent trips to the humor section of your local bookstore. I have been told that the first rule of comedy is "If you can't make your own funny, steal someone else's." Help yourself to the humorously skewed visions of people like Dave Barry, Bill Cosby, Paul Reiser, and others like them. (Loretta LaRoache is a motivational speaker who, both in person and in her book *Relax—You May Have Only a Few Minutes Left: Using the Power of Humor to Overcome Stress in Your Life and Work*, does a very funny job of showing how humor can help you get out of your own way and get what you want out of life.)

Likewise, get in the habit of bringing more comedy into your life by watching funny videos, going to comedy clubs, and reading the authors recommended above and others like them. By apprenticing with the masters, you can begin to learn how to use your own sense of humor as a powerful weapon for beating off the stress gremlins,

whose greatest pleasure is stealing the joy from your life
and relationships.

4. See God in the little things.

My wife has a pet name for God. She calls him "The God
of the Gym Door."

In high school, for various reasons common to all
adolescent girls, she often ran behind schedule. A monitor
at the front door of her school would give students demerits
if they came in past a certain time, even if they weren't
late for first period. The only options available on the days
she was late were to take the demerit or be creative and
try the gym door. The gym door was conveniently located
off the parking lot, but under most circumstances it was
locked. As my wife tells it, though, on those days that she
absolutely positively had to be there, and she remembered
to pray about it, somehow the gym door was always open
for her.

This might sound silly to many of you, and to a point,
it is. But the thing I like to take from this story is that this
God of ours, who loves us so much that even the hairs of
our head are numbered, is not above caring about whether
the gym doors of life are open or not. As God's children,
we need to look for God in the small events of life.

When we thank God for letting us find that good
parking space, or for letting us mail that due bill before
the mail carrier comes, or for the fact that it is a sunny
day, or for the smell of coffee, or for the face of someone
who loves us, we are opening our hearts to joy.

Many of us spend our adulthood cultivating an attitude
we picked up in adolescence, one that demands we act

jaded to be cool. This is absurd. Practicing joy means giving credit where credit is due, and God deserves credit not just for the big times that he pulls our rear ends out of the fire, but for the little acts of kindness he bestows on us every day.

When you pray this evening, and every evening, I would suggest that you write a list of at least five small blessings you encountered during the day. No matter how miserable your day was, look for those little moments and begin thinking of them as brief caresses from the God who loves you enough to stop what he is doing and encourage you in whatever little way he can. Then acknowledge those small hugs with a simple thank-you.

5. Look for ways to make others feel special.
An important part of being a joyful person is finding ways to increase the sense of joy in the people around us. Bringing a smile to the face of the people in our lives is a special joy in and of itself, and nothing brings others a sense of joy as much as knowing that they are special to us, to God, and to others.

We have looked at the importance of acknowledging the simple gifts God gives to us. It is just as important to celebrate the simple gifts others bring to us in the form of their presence, their service, and their insights and obser-vations. One of the best and easiest ways to do this is to say "thank you" for those things others do for us that make our lives easier, whether or not we think they should be doing those things anyway.

For example, when my wife makes dinner, I thank her for it. There are those who would think that's odd. After all, she's a homemaker; isn't that what she is "supposed" to do? I don't think so. The way I see it, anything she does to make my life easier is an act of generosity on her part. She doesn't have to cook. She could say, "I've had it; let's go out today." She could simply feed herself and let us fend for ourselves. She could go out with friends. She could do any number of things.

Those of you who are thinking "No mother would make those other choices" need to do what I do for a day, and you'll see how naive that thought really is. That my wife chooses to stay home and make a meal is something that I need to be grateful for. No, I don't need to throw her a party or give her a medal, but I do need to recognize her generosity with a simple thank-you. This is only one example. My wife and I do this for many things as one simple way to acknowledge the gift that we are to each other.

Of course, there are many other ways to make others feel special. Making a fuss about a person's birthday, anniversary, saint's day, baptism, or any other personal holiday, giving little gifts for no reason, writing notes of appreciation, bringing doughnuts to the office, doing the unexpected thing—all are important ways to make others feel valuable. The point is that when we look for ways to make others' lives easier or more pleasant, we make a gift of our selves, and that is a joyful thing.

6. Take some time to be alone.
I placed this last because I think that our society tends to place too much emphasis on the need to "get away," to "be by myself." Do we really hate what we do and the

people with whom we have chosen to associate so much that we must constantly seek to escape it and them? How sad. People who feel this way about life have bigger problems than a need for "alone time." In fact, if this describes you, no amount of time spent in solitary activities or quiet contemplation will ever be enough, and you will probably fall into an endless pursuit of escapism.

That said, taking time to be alone with your God, your interests, or just your own thoughts is an essential part of joy. Joy is nourished by contemplation, and contemplation is not usually a team sport.

This week, look at your calendar. Each day, carve out at least fifteen minutes for one-on-one time with the Lord, and another fifteen minutes to do something you enjoy doing by yourself. If you can give more time without cheating either the people God has given you to love or the work God has given you to do, then do so. At least once a week, find an additional hour that you can spend in prayer and worship. If you have the opportunity to take a class or find some other way to expand your horizons, then take it.

Just remember that as important as time to yourself is, true joy is not found alone. As philosopher Martin Buber said, "To be is to be in relationship with others." And as God himself said in the book of Genesis, "It is not good for the man to be alone" (Genesis 2:18). God made people for each other, and true joy is found by entering more deeply into the intimate community of people, a community that foreshadows our membership in the communion of saints. In other words, we get ready for the joy of heaven not by being alone and craving escape, but by pursuing and rejoicing in all the messy joy of intimacy with all of the people God has so generously placed in our lives.

The Gift of Joy

Joy is a gift, and Christians of all stripes, especially Catholics, are called to unwrap that gift with relish. Scripture says: "Rejoice in the Lord always. I shall say it again: rejoice!" (Philippians 4:4). Sadly, many Christians think of joy as an uncomfortable add-on that reeks of self-indulgence. I hope we have done something in this chapter to dispel that odd, sad, and frankly unspiritual notion.

Joy plays an essential role in the life of the Christian, and one of the major benefits is insulation from the slings and barbs that attack our peace both from within and without. Those who ignore joy do so at their peril. Those who practice it, truly fostering their sense of joy, will come to know God in all his providential glory, and experience the "peace beyond all understanding" that results.

8

Walk through the Fire

Some people imagine that one day, with practice, they will be able to float above all the cares and worries of life. They will become gurus of sorts who will attain complete and total inner peace.

This is an illusion.

No matter how well developed our mental and spiritual defenses are, there will be times when we feel stressed and anxious. But even in the face of inescapable stress, God can help us claim victory. First we must learn to walk through the fire.

Too many of us stand outside the flames, knowing that we must go forward but fearing that we cannot. As a result, we live in constant fear—fear of moving forward, fear of standing still. Just as Shadrach, Meshach, and Abednego could stand in the furnace of Babylon and not be harmed because the presence of God was with them, we too must be willing to be thrown into the fire of life's problems. Confident that the Lord is at our side, we have nothing to fear.

God Never Leads Backward

MICHAEL, AN ENGINEER, LOST HIS JOB after twenty-five years of working for the
same company. A new company acquired his firm and replaced all
of the midlevel managers with its own people. Though recognized
as an expert by his colleagues, Michael was one of the few people in
his field who did not have a college degree. Despite his significant
experience, other companies refused to even consider his resume.
He was devastated.

———

When Michael first called me he was extremely depressed, and
many false thoughts were clouding his thinking. "No one wants to
hire me. I'm only forty-eight, and I feel like I'm washed up. I don't
know what to do."

Michael was a devoted Catholic who loved the Lord. He was
very angry with God for shaking up his world so fiercely. "Why would
God do this to me? Everything was great for so long. Now, I pray and
I don't feel anything. I am furious that God dumped me like this."

I acknowledged Michael's deep anger and sadness, and over the
course of several meetings, I sat with him while he shared his bit-
terness and hurt. When it was clear that the shock of the tragedy
had begun to wear off and he was ready to begin looking for answers
to the "what next" question, I made a gentle suggestion. I agreed
that while this was certainly a terrible situation and no one except
God ultimately knew what was going to become of him, the one
thing I did know is that when we are thrown into the fire, we must
make a choice. We can either respond in a false way and be consumed by the flames, or we can respond in a true way by prayerfully
asking God, "How can I use this challenge you have sent to lead
me to a more abundant life?"

God never moves backward. He only leads us further up and into deeper trust of his perfect love and providence. When we are thrown into the furnace and watch the security blankets and transitional objects we have been clinging to being consumed by the fire, it is all too natural for us to want to sit down among the flames in bitter disappointment and wait for the fire to take us next. As Christians, we can do much better. Somehow we must find the courage to dance, to sing, to praise God, and ultimately to trust in his deliverance. The key to doing this is asking, "How can I use this challenge, sent by God, to lead me to a more abundant, fulfilling, grace-filled life?"

At first Michael didn't know what to do with this question. He understood that I wasn't being insensitive to his pain, because I had taken time to really listen to him and understand his experience before making this suggestion; but he just didn't know how to answer it. I asked him to do the following: Every time he felt like complaining to God, he could, but he had to add this petition to his complaint—"Show me how to use this terrible loss to lead me to a more abundant life."

Gradually, Michael began formulating a plan. He liked his job, especially for the security that it provided, but he had not felt challenged in it for a long time. He told me that he had always wanted to own his own business, but he had been too afraid to try. He did not know much about running a business, didn't even know what kind of business he wanted to start. I suggested that he leave all the doors open to God—continue looking for a position but put more energy than he ever had before into thinking and acting on his secret wish.

As we draw closer to God, he causes us to face the fears that stand between us and him. While he gives us the grace to claim victory, we must fight the battle with the gifts he has given. In other words, he will equip us, but he will not do it for us.

The more Michael prayed, the more apparent it became that God wanted him to give up his fear of insecurity. Michael had turned to his job for security, but God wanted more. It was time to trust that God could provide a more fulfilling life than any job ever could. Through prayer, Michael felt God leading him more seriously into the option of starting his own business.

Being a remarkable woman, Michael's wife promised to support Michael in whatever he felt God was leading him to do. All she asked was that he include her in the entire process so that she could really be a partner to him. One weekend the two of them went to a franchise fair where they found a business that appealed to both of them. After more prayer and several anxious nights, they decided to take out a second mortgage on their home and procure a Small Business Administration loan to pay for the start-up costs.

They were terrified, but they knew that as they prayed and weighed their options it was the only choice God had shown them that seemed to hold out the promise for a more abundant life. So they took it.

Michael recently called me to share what had happened since then. "It's been a wild ride," he said, "but my wife and I have never felt more blessed. We are opening a second location of the business, I am being challenged in new ways, and I just feel so much more alive. My wife and I are working together as we never could have when I was doing the old job.

"Thanks for helping me figure out what God was doing to me and why. I look back now and see that I was so lost before. I can't believe it, but I'm actually grateful God took me away from all of that now."

Believe it, folks. Christ came that you might have life and have it more abundantly.

A Life Built on Wisdom

When I talk about pursuing a more abundant life, I am not talking about chasing after more money or a bigger house or any other kind of worldly success. Ultimately, I am talking about pursuing a life built on wisdom and trust in God's love and providence. But when we pursue that, other rewards often follow. In the Book of Wisdom, King Solomon observes:

> *Therefore I prayed, and prudence was given me;*
>> *I pleaded, and the spirit of Wisdom came to me.*
> *I preferred her to scepter and throne,*
> *And deemed riches nothing in comparison with her,*
>> *nor did I liken any priceless gem to her;*
> *Because all gold, in view of her, is a little sand,*
>> *and before her, silver is to be accounted mire.*
> *Beyond health and comeliness I loved her,*
> *And I chose to have her rather than the light,*
>> *because the splendor of her never yields to sleep.*
> *Yet all good things together came to me in her company,*
>> *and countless riches at her hands;*
> *And I rejoiced in them all, because Wisdom is their leader,*
>> *though I had not known that she is the mother of these.*
>> *Wisdom 7:7–12*

Wisdom is the constant pursuit of answers that will lead us to a fuller life, a life that places God at the center. It's a life that prefers the wisdom that comes from God's mouth more than anything else—more than the security that comes from money, the stability that comes from a certain position or station, or the comfort we get from certain relationships.

As the above Scripture shows us, Solomon observed the great irony that when we choose only wisdom, many things come with it. Likewise, we do well to remember Jesus' words: "But seek first the kingdom [of God] and his righteousness, and all these things will be given you besides" (Matthew 6:33). We do not pursue the blessings; we pursue God. And when we truly pursue God, he in his generosity will give us all we truly need to live the full life we long for, a life of peace, joy, grace, healing, and wholeness, filled with meaningful relationships and meaningful work.

I know at least a hundred stories as encouraging as Michael's. I have encountered people who have lost their jobs, their health, or their loved ones, as well as scores of individuals who simply had to face the fear of not knowing what to do next. I have had the pleasure of working with these individuals to help them discover how to face the traumas, crises, and challenges they encounter and how to discover the door to a more abundant life.

Don't Be Troubled

In 1530 our Lady appeared to a Mexican peasant named Juan Diego. She asked him to go to the bishop and request that a church be built in her honor. The bishop, who I am sure was used to dealing with more than his share of religious kooks, asked for a sign. In a subsequent vision, our Lady directed Juan Diego to go to a place where he would find roses, though it was not the season for them. He was to gather the roses in his cloak and present them to the bishop.

Having done as he was told and finding everything just as our Lady said he would, he brought the roses to the bishop. When he opened his *tilpa*, he presented another surprise to His Excellency: the beautiful and dramatic portrait of the Blessed Mother we know as Our Lady of Guadeloupe. It is a portrait that exists even to this day, despite having been created on a cloak made of typically very brittle cactus fibers.

"That's nice, Greg. So what?" you might be tempted to ask.

Well, while many people know that story, what they may not know is what the Blessed Mother told Juan Diego personally. She gave him a message that is as important today as it was five hundred years ago: "Do not let yourself be bothered by anything."

I began this book with an examination of our prayer that the Lord would "protect us from all anxiety" and his command to "Be not afraid!" I would like to wrap up our discussion with these words of the Blessed Mother: "Do not let yourself be troubled by anything."

It is true. You will *feel* afraid, you will *feel* stress, and sometimes you will *feel* so anxious that you will think you are going to pop. But what does that matter? As long as we have discerned the true path, the path that leads to a more abundant life, then nothing else matters. We can feel the fear and do it anyway, because we know that if God is for us, then nothing can be against us. As the old Quaker hymn says, "No storm can shake my inmost calm, while to that Rock I'm clinging." Feeling afraid is different from *being* afraid, which would mean that a person acted on the fear he felt.

We can accomplish a great deal in life even if we feel nervous, stressed, or afraid while we do it. Ask any people who have done brave things, and they will tell you that they were terrified the entire time. What makes people brave is their ability to feel afraid and do what needs to be done anyway.

At the same time, the more we do what is true regardless of how fearful we are, the less we fear in the future. God provides what we need to challenge our fear, and he rewards our efforts to overcome our anxieties by giving us greater peace. He just needs us to take that first step. He needs us to step into the fire, trusting that our lives will become richer for the experience.

A Plan for Abundant Living

Take a moment to consider your life. Do you feel trapped? Claustrophobic? Does it seem as if the walls of your world are closing in on you? Do you ever wonder if this is all there is? Then it is long past time for you to shake things up a bit.

All of these feelings come from not having taken up the challenge to live in the truth and pursue a more abundant life. If your actions, choices, and priorities lead you into greater competence, intimacy, strength, hope, and joy, then you are living in the truth. If not, then it is time to change.

Consider the following questions with an eye to creating a plan for living a more abundant life.

1. If you woke up tomorrow and the people and circumstances of your life were the same but God had granted you the miracle of being able to respond to these people and situations more successfully, with real power, strength, assertiveness, and love, what specific things would you do differently?

2. What would it take to make you feel more alive every day? Avoid the temptation to answer this question in an escapist way. In other words, don't ask yourself what it would take to have more fun or "get away" more. Rather, ask what would it take for you to enjoy the people in your life more, to command more respect from those people, or to serve them more joyfully.

3. What kind of work, tasks, activities, or learning opportunities do you feel you must take on to live life more abundantly? While keeping in mind the commitments you have

made to the important people in your life, how can you begin to take some small steps to participate in these new activities today?

Resist the temptation to think that you must do it *all* right now. You can't, and you will burn out trying. Likewise, resist the temptation to think that you cannot pursue these interests at all right now. You must do *something* to begin working toward these goals, but it would be better for you to take small, steady steps. Ten minutes a day of pursuing these goals is much better than no time at all, and sometimes ten minutes a day is even healthier than pursuing these goals eight or more hours a day.

Balance is key. Resist the lie of polarized thinking that tells you that you must be able to do it totally or not do it at all. This is how Satan stops people from acting in the first place or, if they are acting, causes them to do so in a way that is disrespectful to the commitments they have made to the important people in their life. By neither doing too little, nor too much, we pursue the golden mean, that healthy middle way that keeps us moving toward the destination God wishes for us, but in a manner that keeps apace of God's timing for our lives.

4. What personal obstacles stand between you and the pursuit of this more abundant life? Do you lack knowledge? If so, what steps must you begin taking today to acquire that knowledge? Do you lack personal strength? Wisdom? Assertiveness? Other personal traits that would increase your chances of success? If so, what kind of counsel will you seek to help you develop and nurture these strengths? Are you too undisciplined to pursue your goals effectively? If so,

how will you arrange for the accountability you need to keep yourself on track?

5. What objections will the people in your life present to your pursuit of these personal or relational goals? What steps can you take to minimize the negative effects on others that may come from following the call to live more abundantly? (Incidentally, if you are not being escapist, the pursuit of these goals should actually build intimacy.) For example, will you need to adjust your active pursuit to take into account important promises or commitments you have already made? Will you need to seek relationship counseling to find respectful ways to work together effectively?

Step into the Fire

The above are some very big questions. We cannot use the fact that we do not immediately know the answers as an excuse for not asking the questions. Psychologists speak of the "actualizing drive," the innate call to become the person God created each of us to be, which is part and parcel of being human. When we embrace the challenge of our actualizing tendency, we pick up our cross and follow the Lord, and we can experience the Resurrection that follows. By contrast, when we try to ignore the call, we never pick up the cross or experience the Resurrection because we are too afraid the cross will be too heavy, that it will give us splinters, that maybe we won't rise in the end after all, that people will laugh at us or criticize us along the way, that we might trip and get dirty, or worse.

The funny thing is that the pain involved in this sort of dithering is so much worse than the pain that comes from actually carrying the cross, largely because it is a pain that never ends. There is no resurrection, only fretting about whether there ever would be. Too many people waste the majority of their lives living this sort of half-life. This is not what Christ calls us to.

It is my hope that the tools presented throughout this book will help you begin to get your fears, anxieties, and stresses under control to the degree that you can then take a deep breath and jump into the fire, trusting that God will take care of the part that you can't handle. But don't think for one minute that the techniques presented in this or any other book, or the relief promised by some pill or other means, will ever eliminate your anxiety completely. Don't wait to act until all of your anxiety is gone, or you will be waiting a very long time.

Jesus said, "He who loves his life will lose it." When we try to live a life that is small enough for us to manage comfortably, our life becomes smaller and smaller until it disappears because, quite frankly, we are incapable of managing even the tiniest life on our own. But when we love God first, and then throw ourselves on his mercy as we pursue his truth, then we will begin to live and live more abundantly.

Step into the fire—the refiner's fire—and let the Holy Spirit make you into finest gold that you may be a witness to the power of Christ's transforming love and transformative power.

Hear the words of the Son of God calling to your fearful, still soul. Feel his power as he stands at the foot of your self-imposed sick bed and proclaims, "Get up! Your faith has healed you. I came that you might have life and live it more abundantly. Stand up, walk, and live!"

A WORD FROM THE AUTHOR

The Pastoral Solutions Institute
Catholic Answers for Life's Toughest Questions
234 St. Joseph Dr.
Steubenville, Ohio 43952
(740) 266-6461
www.exceptionalmarriages.com

"Marriage and family counseling agencies by their specific work of guidance and prevention . . . offer valuable help in rediscovering the meaning of love and life, and in supporting every family in its mission as the 'sanctuary of life.'"

~POPE JOHN PAUL II
From The Gospel of Life

Dear Friends,
I hope you enjoyed this book, but everyone needs a little help from time to time. If you are struggling to apply your faith to marriage, family, or personal problems, ***The Pastoral Solutions Institute*** can help.

Through the Institute, I work with an advisory board of solidly Catholic psychotherapists, theologians, and physicians who specialize in finding Catholic answers to life's difficult questions.

Our effective telephone-counseling program and dynamic seminars incorporate cutting-edge psychology and orthodox Catholic theology to help you find peace in your life. The Institute has helped hundreds of people just like you who are coping with marriage and family problems, depression and anxiety, sexual issues, problem habits, grief and loss, parenting questions, and ethical dilemmas.

Call today for more information on counseling, seminars, books, parish enrichment, and professional training. Let us help you brighten your world with the healing light of Christ.

Yours in Christ,
Gregory K. Popcak, MSW, LCSW
Director
The Pastoral Solutions Institute